Wandering Woman: Ohio
The Ultimate Road Trip: One Woman's Journey Across the United States by RV

Julie Bettendorf

Contents

Introduction

Are you sure? I thought to myself, as I tried not to panic. I was a long way from anything familiar, but that was how it should be. I had driven thousands of miles on dusty, pothole-filled roads. It's often on the worst roads that you can discover something truly amazing.

My dusty CRV was parked beside me, containing one restless dog and a variety of snack bags, all empty by now. There were no buildings in sight, no cars or people or movement at all. Only the constant humming of the insects as they buzzed around my head.

I turned to my left – another straight road that trailed off into the distance. I glanced over to the right, then behind me – two more barely discernible roads stretched out into the abyss. I was in a four-way intersection with no signs, no sense of direction, and no sign of life for several miles. No cell service either. *Damn*, I thought. *I'm lost.*

How did I get here? I couldn't help but feel like this little intersection was a cruel metaphor for life. I began to daydream, imagining each road might transport me back to a different time, a different role in my life, and a different me.

If I took the road from whence I came, it could lead me all the way back to Oregon, back to my cheating third husband, back to a life of loneliness and solitude. There is no greater loneliness than being married to someone who isn't actually present in your life.

If I took the road to my left, perhaps it could take me back to my career as a dental hygienist, a job I hated deep down in my soul. There is something so disengaging about cleaning teeth for a living. It's a disgusting, smelly way to get a paycheck. It pays well, which is great, but the best part is the huge gob of friends I enjoy to this day.

Or maybe the road to my right, *yes – maybe that's the path*, I imagined. Maybe it could take me back to my real treasure, my kids. Back to their smiling, innocent faces as toddlers, as they danced around the Christmas tree and their father and I were still married. Back when they still needed me for every little thing.

But, that was just it. I didn't feel needed anymore. My kids weren't toddlers anymore – they were both full-grown adults, and far too busy for me. My dental buddies were still working, but I wasn't. Dental hygiene had robbed me of the cartilage in my fingers, giving me severe, disabling arthritis. And, I wouldn't be returning to any more husbands either, because three marriages were quite enough for me.

All three of these paths, all three of these roles – the wife, the mother, and the dental hygienist – had seemingly been stripped from me within a year. I was lost and looking to find myself again.

The funny thing about this phrase, "not all who wander are lost" – is that, in my experience, wandering and being lost walk hand-in-hand with one another, and the expression can be flipped. In my experience, not all who are lost are wandering, and that is a real disservice to the beauty and clarity that the world has to offer.

When one becomes lost, wandering is the only option to guide oneself back to a path. After all, one could not come upon any dirt path at all without wandering.

I began wandering at an early age, both with my mind and with my feet. At eight years old, I was reading a book about archaeology and dreaming of one day seeing Egypt. I didn't follow a traditional path in high school either, going heavily into foreign languages, in hopes of one day using them.

At twenty-five years old, I divorced my first husband (the dental student who talked me into becoming a dental hygienist so I could work for him) and decided to give traveling a real shot. I took off for the Andes and Macchu Picchu, climbing up ancient Inca stone steps to reach the magnificent ruins.

Anyone who has been to Macchu Picchu will tell you there is something ethereal and deeply spiritual about the place. The ruins stretch out across the emerald green mountains, way up in the middle of the sky. Macchu Picchu gave me my first experience of feeling history. This trip inspired me to come back and complete a degree in archaeology, and I've been wandering ever since.

More travel followed including a backpack trip around Europe for three months, by myself, and trips to Britain, Italy, and Greece. I visited the burial places of Crusaders, mummies, and ancient kings. I happened upon the castle of my namesake in Bettendorf, Luxembourg, and wandered my way through European history.

My favorite excursion by far was finally seeing Egypt with my daughter in 2012. Just like my childhood dream envisioned, I rode a camel beneath the pyramids of Giza, with my head wrapped in some man's sweaty turban. It was perfect.

Traveling has always been my own personal antidote to pain. I went to Mexico after my first and second divorces, Canada after my third, and Italy after my dad died. Call it avoidance if you want, but I call it an accelerated form of healing in the purest sense of the word. I believe travel can heal your soul.

Wandering has always worked its wonders on me – made me feel renewed, rejoiceful, grateful, and purposeful. It's been my medicine.

So, as I stood in that intersection, I once again wondered how wandering had led me so astray this time. *What the hell am I supposed to do now?* It was then that I realized that one last path had not been considered yet – the path which stretched straight out in front of me. *Which role does this represent?* I pondered.

The answer smacked me in the face.

That last dirt road – the only path that could take me where I wanted to go, the only path that ever truly healed me or showed me the way – was the path of the traveler. The wife, the mother, and the hygienist roles – though valued in their time – were sitting in the bleachers now. It was time to welcome and enable my boldest, bravest, and perhaps most pivotal role yet:

The role of the Wandering Woman.

Welcome to Wandering Woman

This book is for you – the grieving empty nester mom, the begrudged housewife, the woman in need of a drastic change in her life. Really, this book is for anyone with a passion for traveling. If you feel lost with no sense of direction or purpose in life, that's a bonus – this book will be even more appealing to you. And lastly, if you're a man reading this book, congratulations for holding a book with the word woman in the title. You're contributing to gender equality, and that's pretty neat.

I decided to combine three of my dearest loves – travel, history, and archaeology – and put them into a book because I believe wandering has the power to change your life. I have been to many areas of the world and have enjoyed too many outstanding experiences to list. However, by the time both my children moved out in 2017, I realized I was a stranger in my own country. It was the perfect time to explore a new country (my own) and discover a new me at the same time. I have been traveling for seven years now, and I've upgraded to a small RV. I also have a new traveling companion, another sweet Sheltie, named Rosie. ***Wandering Woman*** is the chronicle of my journey across the United States, discovering the joy of getting lost and finding myself along the way.

Why You Need to Take a Road Trip

*A*merica, *the beautiful?* I sure think so, but I didn't realize just how beautiful our country is until I embarked on traveling across the United States, full time, in a small RV.

The United States offers something for everyone. From spectacular beaches, austere mountains, to rolling plains, our country has it all. It's difficult to comprehend just how large and impressive our scenery is, until you experience it first-hand, with the ultimate road trip.

I also realized just how much of our history is missing from U.S. history I was taught as a kid. The history of our country didn't begin with the pilgrims landing on Plymouth Rock in the 1600s. Our history is far more ancient, with rock art and archaeological sites dating back over 12,000 years.

We owe a tremendous debt to early pioneers who tamed our land. The Mormons and other groups ventured into the great unknown with their families and their worldly possessions. Some of them pulled cumbersome handcarts across the country to settle in inhospitable, dangerous locations.

The goal of ***Wandering Woman*** is to bring history back to life and make it interesting again. I am presenting some famous sites, and many little-known ones. You will take the road-less-traveled with me, while we explore ghost towns, rock art sites, archaeological sites, and museums, to discover the colorful tapestry that is our country.

I present some history, including dates, but my goal is to present more of the real-life stories of history, including ghost stories, profiles in history, voices from the past, and moments in time, to give you, the reader, a deeper understanding of the context of history.

This is by no means an exhaustive list of places to visit. In fact, I encourage you to discover America for yourself, as I am doing, by making a trek across the land by car or RV. You can venture forth as the early explorers did, just a little more comfortably, with a lot less hardship.

I hope you enjoy this book and take a little time out to discover our beautiful country, and maybe even discover yourself in the process.

Safe Travels,

Julie Bettendorf

Welcome to Ohio
The Buckeye State

Ohio is an ancient land, full of surprising and majestic archaeological sites like the Great Serpent Mound. Ohio is also home to early settlers from Europe, which is evident from sites like Schoenbrunn Village. Ohio is at the center of everything, including the Underground Railroad, which helped slaves escape to freedom in Canada. Ohio needs to be experienced slowly to fully taste the flavor of this amazing state.

Five Things to Love about Ohio:

- Early military sites like Fort Recovery and Fort Steuben

- Amazing eclectic museums like Campus Martius Museum

- Quaint historic towns like Gallipolis

- Ancient earthworks like Mound City

- Famous Underground Railroad sites like John Rankin House

Dreams of Ohio

"As a boy, because I was born and raised in Ohio, about 60 miles north of Dayton, the legends of the Wrights have been in my memories as long as I can remember." **Neil Armstrong**

"In my neighborhood in Springfield, Ohio, there were a lot of young kids. We all played tackle football after school, but I knew very early on that I was not an athlete." **John Legend**

"As a defense attorney in Ohio, my dad would accept food in lieu of money from his poorer clients, and work into the night as if he were being paid in bullion instead of sweet potato pies." **Cord Jefferson**

Famous People from Ohio

Neil Armstrong, astronaut, 1930–2012

George Armstrong Custer, Calvary Commander, 1839–1876

Clark Gable, actor, 1901–1960

John Glenn, astronaut, 1921–2016

Ulysses S. Grant, 18th President of the U.S., Civil War General, 1822–1885

Paul Newman, actor, philanthropist, 1925–2008

Annie Oakley, sharpshooter, folk hero, 1860–1926

Early Ohio

Early Ohio Residents

Early Ohio Resident

Archaeological Dig at Fort Laurens

Fort Recovery

F_ort Recovery_ is the site of a battle on November 4, 1791, during which 1300 men, under the leadership of Territorial Governor, General Arthur St. Clair, were overcome by over 1400 warriors from nine tribes. Under the leadership of Chief Little Turtle, they were able to surround St. Clair in about fifteen minutes. Almost 1000 of St. Clair's people, including two-thirds of the officers, women and children were killed.

A new fort was built on the site in 1793, and during construction, skeletal remains were discovered, including over 600 skulls. The remains are reinterred in a mass grave.

Another battle occurred here in 1794, during which General Anthony Wayne's forces were victorious over the Shawnee, Delaware, Ottawa, Miami, and Ojibwa Indians. This battle led to the Treaty of Greenville in 1795, an agreement forcing indian nations to give up most of their land in Ohio.

Today, as you walk around the site, you can see a stockade, block-houses, and log structures, including a tool house and pioneer cabin.

Part of the Fort Recovery historic area is a large obelisk which commemorates the burial vault of the men killed in the Battle of the Wabash and the Battle of Fort Recovery.

Fort Recovery also has a wonderful museum containing battle and pioneer artifacts.

How to get to Fort Recovery:

Fort Recovery is located at One Fort Site Street in Fort Recovery, Ohio

Profiles in history:

Major General Arthur Sinclair was born in Scotland in 1734 into a life of privilege. At 30, he received an officer's commission in the British Army. He emigrated to North America, married, and became a wealthy landowner in Pennsylvania.

He was acquitted of a court-martial for abandoning Fort Ticonderoga, leaving him in debt. St. Clair was elected to Congress, and became governor of the Northwest Territory. He signed several treaties with Native Americans in the Ohio Valley.

Voices from the past:

"The United States will deceive themselves, if they think an insignificant, and undisciplined army, badly provided, will conquer the formidable enemy they are now at war with. They are numerous-they are trained warriors and are elated with victory and plunder." **Officer from the conflict, as stated in the Maryland Journal, December 30, 1791.**

Shrum Mound

S_hrum Mound_ is a Native American burial mound created by the Adena Culture, who lived in the Ohio Valley from 800 BC to 100 AD.

The mound is approximately 2000 years old, and is 20 feet high
and has a diameter of 100 feet.

Shrum Mound is named after the Shrum family, who donated the land to the Ohio Historical Society. In 2015, the Ohio History Connection removed 18 trees from the top of the mound, to help prevent damage.

How to get to Shrum Mound:

Shrum Mound is located at 3141 McKinley Avenue, in Columbus, Ohio.

Schoenbrunn Village

Lovely ***Schoenbrunn Village*** was founded on May 3, 1772, by Moravian missionaries. It began as a Delaware Indian mission during the 1770s, and later became Ohio's first organized settlement. The name "Schoenbrunn" means beautiful spring in German.

What you see today is a reconstruction of the original town and mission. Missions were laid out in the form of a cross.

David Zeisberger, the founder of the town, described several streets and about 60 buildings within the original town. He also mentions the presence of several Indian mounds in his diary.

As you walk around the town, you can see the Anton Cabin. He was a native helper who tutored Zeisberger in the Delaware language. Anton died of yellow fever and is buried in Gods' Acre Cemetery.

The Conners Cabin belonged to Richard Conner, a hunter and trapper who discovered a young white girl in a Shawnee camp. He wanted to marry the girl, so he gave the chief $200 and their first born child. The son, James Conner, was the first white boy born in Ohio. He was given to the chief. James was ransomed back when he was 4 for 40 buckskins.

The Jungmann Cabin belonged to the inn keeper for the village,
Visiting missionaries could stay with him.

You can also see the Zeisberger Cabin, belonging to Moravian missionary, David Zeisberger, the founder of Schoenbrunn. He wanted to teach the Indians about Christianity, but not interfere with their way of life. Zeisberger created translations of English and German into the Delaware language. He married when he was 60.

The church contained the first bell in Ohio, and could hold 330-500 people.

Don't miss the school, where students were grouped in choirs, with the same age and gender. The Delaware saw their language first written down in this school.

God's Acre is the original cemetery. Residents of Schoenbrunn were buried facing east, so they could see the savior when he returned. The original wood markers were replaced by stone.

How to get to Schoenbrunn Village:

Schoenbrunn Village is located at 1984 E. High Avenue, in New Philadelphia, Ohio.

A moment in time:

Next to the peaceful town of Schoenbrunn, there is Gnadenhutten. When I walked around Gnadenhutten, it was covered in mist, giving the historic place an ethereal quality. A bloody event happened here on March 8, 1782. American militiamen gathered 96 Native American men, women, and children who were harvesting corn in Gnadenhutten. The militia murdered the entire group. leaving their mutilated bodies lying on the ground. Today you can see the memorial to the victims, a small mission house, and a cooper's shop.

Fort Laurens

***F**ort Laurens* was built in 1778, during the Revolutionary War. Although there are no original buildings remaining, you can sense the historical significance of the site.

Fort Laurens was named after Henry Laurens, the president of the Second Continental Congress. The British soon learned of the fort's construction and laid siege to the fort in 1779.

The siege lasted four weeks before American reinforcements arrived. The fort was abandoned in August of that year. The remains of the fort were destroyed when the Ohio and Erie Canal was built in 1832.

During archaeological excavations, a mass grave was discovered, containing soldiers killed during the siege. One of these soldiers was given a full military burial and interred in the Tomb of the Unknown Patriot of the American Revolution at Fort Laurens. Others were placed in a crypt contained in the museum's wall.

Today you can visit an excellent museum on the site.

How to get to Fort Laurens:

Fort Laurens is located at 11067 Fort Laurens Rd, NW, in Bolivar, Ohio.

Voices from the past:

"The siege lasted 4 weeks, provisions exhausted; finally for 3 or 4 days had to live on half a biscuit a day-then the last two days washed their moccasins and broiled them for food, and broiled strips of old dried hides." **Captain Benjamin Biggs, 1779.**

Zoar Village

I dyllic ***Zoar Village*** was established in 1817 by 200 German separatists who came from Wurttemberg. They fled their native country to gain religious freedom. The village was named after the biblical city of Zoar, which Lot fled to. Zoar means a place of refuge.

The settlers held the land as a community, with everything held in common. The village prospered, becoming self sustaining within 20 years. The settlers were even able to export some goods for a profit. By 1850, the village was worth over $1 million dollars.

From 1822 to 1829, Zoar residents helped build the Ohio and Erie Canal. It was a period of celibacy so the women could work on the canal instead of having children.

The town is laid out with a town square, and farmland surrounding the buildings. The gardens in Zoar are carefully planned out, with a center tree representing Christ, and surrounded by a hedge representing heaven.

The twelve trees surrounding the center are the apostles. The numerous paths represent the paths of life, with the perimeter path representing the world.

As you walk around this delightful town, you can't miss the Zoar Hotel, built in 1833. During its heyday, the hotel housed artists, families, and famous figures including President William McKinley.

One of my favorite buildings is the quaint tin shop, built in 1825. The town also had its own brewery, just like many old German towns.

Other important buildings in Zoar Village include the Inn on the River, built in 1829, and the number one house, built in 1835.

This magnificent building was once the home of Joseph Bimeler, the founder of Zoar. He died in 1853, and the town declined. In 1898, the town dissolved as a community.

How to get to Zoar Village:

Zoar Village is located in East Central Ohio, about 16 miles south of Canton and 3 miles east of I-77 near Bolivar.

Ghost story:

In 1832, a man who was traveling on a canal boat near Zoar became very sick and was dropped off near the Inn by the River. The man died from his sickness and was buried by the good people of Zoar. A woman came looking for the man, saying that he was her husband and that he had money sewn into his coat. She wanted his body exhumed.

The good people of Zoar refused, so the woman found herself a man for hire, to dig up the body. She found the money sewn into the coat of the dead man. She took the money and the body was reburied. After the woman left, cholera broke out and killed many of the Zoar residents. The woman and the man she hired both died of cholera on the canal boat when they left town. It is said the dead man haunts the Inn to this day.

Newark Earthworks

The ***Newark Earthworks*** was built by the Hopewell culture between 100 AD and 400 AD. The complex spreads out over 4 square miles, with walls up to 14 feet high.

The site consists of three sections, the Great Circle Earthworks, Octagon Earthworks, and Wright Earthworks.

The Great Circle Earthworks has a diameter of 1200 feet and consists of a 5 foot deep moat surrounded by 8 foot walls. Buffalo Bill brought his wild west show to the area in 1884.

The Octagon Earthworks functioned as an ancient observatory to track lunar paths.

The Wright Earthworks is a square enclosure. Large sections of this earthwork were destroyed to construct the Ohio Canal in the 19th century.

How to get to Newark Earthworks:

The Newark Earthworks are located at 455 Hebron Rd. in Heath, Ohio,

A helpful timeline:

The various periods of occupation in early North America can be confusing. Don't be surprised if you read slightly different dates from other sources, but these are some general guidelines to know about:

- The Paleo-Indian Period, from 10,000 to 8500 BC, is characterized by hunting and gathering, and small family groups in temporary camps. Artifacts from this period include spears and darts.

- The Archaic Period, from 8500 to 500 BC, is characterized by some cultivation, and small base settlements. Artifacts from this period include stone, shell, and copper items.

- The Early Woodland Period, from 500 BC to 1 AD, is characterized by permanent villages, organization under a tribal or religious leader, elite burials in mounds. Artifacts from this period include the addition of clay pottery.

- The Middle Woodland Period, from 1 AD to 400 AD, is characterized by the introduction of maize, long-distance trade, and elite burials with precious objects. Burial mounds, platform mounds, and earthworks were built.

- The Late Woodland Period, from 400 AD to 800 AD, is characterized by cultivated seed plants, large permanent villages, and use of the bow and arrow.

- The Early Mississippi Period, from 800 AD to 1300 AD, is characterized by cultivation of corn, beans, and squash, with permanent villages and farming settlements. Temples and houses of leaders were built on mounds in major villages. Pottery and artistic forms were developed.

- The Late Mississippi Period, from 1300 AD to 1700 AD, is characterized by towns enclosed in stockade walls, increased power among chiefs and religious leaders. Increased and more elaborate artistic representations on pottery, shells, and wood.

Fort Ancient Earthworks

Magnificent ***Fort Ancient Earthworks*** is North America's largest hilltop enclosure and was built 2000 years ago. It was used as a sacred space by the Fort Ancient Culture.

Six trails take you through various sections of the earthworks. You can drive up to scenic overlooks, stone rings, circles, and other features.

You drive through an area known as the Great Gateway, which travels through a section of the earthworks, and you can see how massive the structure is.

Fort Ancient has a wonderful museum containing many artifacts excavated from the area and surrounding sites.

My favorite artifacts are the numerous pieces created from mica, a shiny, glass-like material.

How to get to Fort Ancient Earthworks:

Fort Ancient Earthworks is located at 6123 State Route 350, in Oregonia, Ohio.

A word about cultures, traditions, and periods:

- A culture is a specific social group with a unique way of life. An example is the Adena culture, identified by conical burial mounds, copper artifacts, and specific shapes of beads and pipes.

- A tradition, is a broadly identified way of life, in use by different cultures at different time periods. The Woodland Tradition can be identified across many cultures in many geographic locations. Woodland tradition is identified by the beginning of agriculture, potter making, and the establishment of permanent villages.

- A period, is a specified span of time during which one tradition is dominant. The Woodland Tradition has several periods including the burial mound period of 1000 BC to 700 AD. A period is a method of measuring time.

John Rankin House

T he delightful *John Rankin House* is perched high atop a hill. This small, unassuming structure was a key location for the Underground Railroad.

The house was built in 1828, and contains four rooms on the ground floor and two bedrooms in the attic. John Rankn and his wife, Jean, moved into the house in 1829.

The house offers a commanding view across the Ohio River. John Rankin placed a light in the front window of the house, to help guide escaped slaves across the river.

Harriett Beecher Stowe visited the house and it became a back-drop for her famous novel, Uncle Tom's Cabin.

How to get to the John Rankin House:

The John Rankin House is located at 6152 Rankin Hill Road, in Ripley, Ohio.

Profiles in history:

John Rankin was born on February 4, 1793, in Dandridge, Tennessee. He became a Presbyterian minister, and one of the most influential "conductors" in helping slaves escape to freedom. He met Jean Lowry while at college and they married in 1816. Jean made her husband's wedding coat, and he made his own shoes. Jean and John Rankin had thirteen children.

Anti-slavery views were not popular in Tennessee, so in 1817, Rankin left Tennessee for good, moving first to Kentucky. His views were not popular in Kentucky either, so he moved to the town of Ripley, in the free state of Ohio, in 1822. Throughout his lifetime, he is estimated to have helped more than 2,000 slaves attain freedom. He also authored numerous letters stating his anti-slavery views. in 1826, the letters were published in a book,

"Letters on American Slavery." John Rankin died on March 18, 1886.

Voices from the past:

"At times attacked on all sides by masters seeking their slaves, John Rankin and his sons beat back their assailant, and held its threshold unsullied." **John Parker, former slave who worked with John Rankin as an Underground Railroad conductor.**

Serpent Mound

T he world-famous *Great Serpent Mound* is an astounding 1348 feet long, 20 feet wide, and 5 feet high, making it the largest effigy mound in the world. The mound forms a gigantic snake with 7 large coils.

The head has open jaws which contain what is believed to be an egg or a frog figure.

Initial radiocarbon dating of the site suggests the serpent mound may have been constructed by the Adena people, over 2300 years ago. However, new research suggests that the serpent mound was, in fact, constructed by the Fort Ancient people around 1100-1400 AD.

The Fort Ancient people commonly depicted serpents as part of their culture and art forms. The Great Serpent was considered to be the Lord of the World Below, a world beneath the Earth's surface.

A burial mound lies about 400 feet from the serpent. This mound was excavated and Adena burial objects were discovered within it. Copper breastplate, stone axes and points, and sandstone pieces with grooves carved into them were found.

How to get to the Great Serpent Mound:

The Great Serpent Mound is located at 3850 State Route 73, in Peebles, Ohio.

A word about the Fort Ancient Culture:

The Fort Ancient Culture was a Native American Culture in the Ohio Valley from 1000 AD to 1750 AD. Fort Ancient Culture sites can be found in Ohio, Indiana, West Virginia, and Kentucky. The Fort Ancient people are credited with bringing maize to Ohio. The Great Serpent Mound represents a constellation known as the Snake. The snake swallows a whole egg, representing a struggle for the benefit of people. Evidence indicates the Great Serpent Mound held special importance for the Fort Ancient people.

There are several phases attributed to Fort Ancient people:

- Early Fort Ancient, from 1000 AD to 1200 AD

- Middle Fort Ancient, from 1200 AD to 1400 AD

- Late Fort Ancient, from 1400 AD to 1750 AD

Campus Martius Museum

T he wonderful ***Campus Martius Museum*** is located in beautiful Marietta, a quaint town founded in 1788 by Rufus Putnam. Marietta was the first organized American settlement in the Northwest Territory.

In 1788, Putnam led his generals from the Revolutionary War across the wilderness and into what is now Ohio. A peace treaty signed in 1795 with Native Americans made town growth possible. The settlement contained an original stockade and was named for an ancient Roman training ground.

The Campus Martius Museum contains a fascinating collection of items from early pioneer life.

The star attraction of the museum is the Rufus Putnam House, preserved intact from the original stockade.

Take your time as you stroll through the house. Interpretive guides will take you on a tour.

How to get to the Campus Martius Museum:

The Campus Martius Museum is located at 601 Second Street, in Marietta, Ohio.

Voices from the past:

"Many of the buildings in Marietta's Historic District date to the city's founding in 1788." **Meriwether Lewis, September 13, 1803.**

Leo Petroglyphs

T he ***Leo Petroglyphs*** are images carved onto a large sand-stone surface. There are 37 images of humans and animals, along with footprints.

The most famous image is that of a human head wearing deer antlers and having bird's feet. This is thought to depict a shaman or supernatural figure.

The Fort Ancient peoples are believed to have carved the images from 1000 AD to 1650 AD. Today, the images are protected under a shelter.

How to get to the Leo Petroglyphs:

The Leo Petroglyphs are located at 357 Township Hwy, in Ray, OH.

A word about petroglyphs and pictographs:

Petroglyphs were made by taking river rock and heating it and then cooling it suddenly so it cracks to form a sharp tool. This tool was used to chisel along with another stone for a hammer to peck or incise the designs on rock. A thick desert coating called a patina was removed to expose the lighter rock underneath.

Pictographs, are painted instead of incised. They are drawn pictures using minerals like hematite mixed with a binder such as animal fat, urine, or oil to make paint.

Pictograph colors are:

- Black, which is made with yellow ochre, pinon gum, and sumac

- Red, which is made with red ochre and mahogany root

- Yellow, which is made with rabbitbrush

- Plant oils and animal fats were used as binders

Gallipolis

***G**allipolis* is a wonderful old French town. In 1790, several hundred French settlers came to the area. They believed they had purchased land, but soon found out they had been cheated.

Some settlers stayed and repurchased the land, settling down and building their homes. They named the city Gallipolis, or City of the Gauls.

About one-third of the settlers died from diseases due to the swampy conditions. The population grew to 1000 people by the 1880s.

Today, Gallipolis is a charming city of parks and quaint buildings next to the Ohio River.

How to get to Gallipolis:

Gallipolis is located in Southeast Ohio about 55 miles southeast of Chillicothe and 44 miles northwest of Charleston, West Virginia.

Our House Tavern

***O**ur House Tavern* is a charming building with a long history. Built in 1819, the tavern has had several famous guests, including General Lafayette, who was entertained in the tavern in 1825.

The tavern contains an enclosed space which would be opened to show that spirits could be served. When the bars were opened up, people could come for a drink. When they were closed, there was either a fight or the Inn was out of drink. This is where the term "bars" came from.

Ladies weren't allowed into the public dining room. The formal dining room was for both ladies and gentlemen. Children eight and younger were fed from their mother's plate. Patrons enjoyed hand painted china, with no two pieces alike. Silver was brought from France.

Ladies could sit in the parlor. which has a fainting chair, for when women couldn't breathe from their corsets.

The ladies bed chamber offered women an opportunity to sleep three women across one bed, at a cost of 75 cents per night. The men's bed chamber offered men an opportunity to sleep on the floor for 25 cents per night, or they could sleep as the women did, with three men to a bed, for 75 cents per night.

There are many unusual features within the tavern. My favorite is a hoof print on the floor, from a patron's horse.

There is also a jacket belonging to Lafayette, who left it there during his visit on may 25, 1825. He spilled something on the jacket and didn't want to keep it.

There is a lovely outdoor kitchen in a separate building. The kitchen has many original artifacts, including a wonderful mouse-trap.

Our House Tavern is reputed to have a few ghosts which inhabit the house and courtyard. They include Henry Cushing, the owner, his daughter, Lucy, foster sister Elizabeth, and singer Jenny Lind.

How to get to Our House Tavern:

Our House Tavern is located at 432 First Avenue in Gallipolis, Ohio.

Mound City

Mound City is a fascinating complex of about two dozen mounds, encompassing an area the size of ten football fields. The city was constructed by the Hopewell, from AD 1 to 400 AD.

The Hopewell didn't live in the enclosure full time. A building was constructed on top of the mounds. After use, the building was dismantled, and then mound construction began. The mounds consist of layers of earth, alternating with layers of clay and sand.

During excavations, 100 cremated remains were found at Mound City. Next to some of the burials, works of art were placed.

There were several important burials at the site, indicating people may have been brought from far away to be ceremonially cremated and buried at Mound City.

One mound contained as many as twenty burials. One grave contained four cremated bodies which were placed on a lining of mica.

Mound City has a wonderful museum containing many artifacts from mound excavations.

My favorite piece is a magnificent projectile point created from crystal quartz.

How to get to Mound City:

Mound City is located at 16062 State Route 104, in Chillicothe, Ohio.

A word about the Hopewell:

The Hopewell were named for Captain Mordecai Hopewell who owned the farm where the first site was excavated in 1891. The Hopewell began about 2000 years ago, and continued for about 500 years, ending 1500 years ago. Some of the mounds created by the Hopewell covered burials. The mounds were built in stages, beginning with a wooden structure housing a clay platform where the burial ceremony was. The dead were cremated or buried. with grave goods placed near the remains. Strings of shells and pearls covered entire skeletons. After the ceremony, the structure was burned or dismantled and then the site was covered with a mound of earth.

The Hopewell traded a wide variety of items and materials, including:

- Copper and silver from the Great Lakes

- Obsidian from the Yellowstone area

- Sharks teeth and seashells from the Atlantic and Gulf of Mexico

- Mica from the Southern Appalachian Mountains

Fort Steuben

***F**ort Steuben* was originally built in 1786, by Major John Francis Hamtramck. The fort you see today is a reconstruction the original fort.

The fort was built to protect surveyors from attacks by the
Shawnee and Delaware tribes and to house 150 men and the
surveyors.

The fort was named after Baron Von Steuben, a Prussian officer serving with George Washingon.

As the men were building the fort, only 33 men could work at the same time, because there weren't enough shoes to go around. The original fort survived until 1790, when it was either burned or dismantled for materials.

Today you can see a reconstructed enlisted men's barracks, hospital, commissary, and guardhouse. The area is also an active archaeological site.

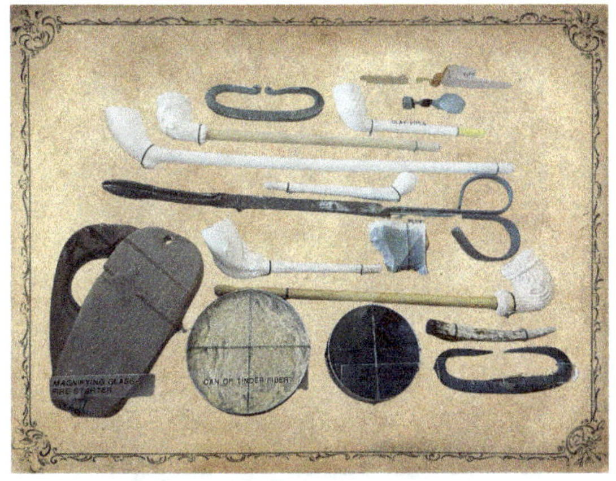

You can enjoy original artifacts recovered at the site.

How to get to Fort Steuben:

Fort Steuben is located at 120 S. Third Street, in Steubenville, Ohio.

Profiles in history:

John Francis Hamtramck was born in Quebec, Canada on August 14th, 1756. He left Canada with the American army when they were forced to withdraw in 1776. In 1783, Hamtramck was ordered to lead and protect a group of surveyors who were tasked with mapping mountain ranges. Hamtramck reasoned that they needed winter lodgings, and began the design of what was to become Fort Steuben. Hamtramck died suddenly in 1803.

Friedrich Wilhelm von Steuben was born in 1730 in Magdeburg, Prussia. he became an officer cadet at 16, and an army lieutenant at 22. Benjamin Franklin met von Steuben in Paris, and enlisted his help with America's struggle for independence. Steuben arrived in Valley Forge in 1778 to train Washington's troops. To award him for his help, Washington promoted von Steuben to Inspector General of the US Army. He became an advisor to Washington from 1789 to 1792. Von Steuben died in 1794, and never went to the fort named after him.

Voices from the past:

" When I drew my sword for the liberties of this country, it was with a determined resolution that nothing but death should make me sheath it before Great Britain had acknowledged the independence of America." **Friedrch Wilhelm von Steuben to Elias Boudinot, December 5, 1782.**

Mound Cemetery

Mound Cemetery is a fascinating place, combining historic burials with a prehistoric mound. The cemetery incorporates a large mound built by the Adena culture from 800 BC to 100 AD.

General Putnam, who was trained as a surveyor, made detailed maps of the mounds in and around Marietta. In 1788, it was decided to preserve the larger mounds. The cemetery was established in 1801 to help preserve the mound.

The founders of the cemetery were Revolutionary War officers and citizens of the Northwest Territory. In fact, the Mound Cemetery has more Revolutionary War officers than any other cemetery in the country.

General Lafayette visited the cemetery in 1825. General Rufus Putnam, the father of Marietta, is buried there, along with Commander Abraham Whipple, Revolutionary War Naval captain, and Ebenezer Sproat, one of the 48 original pioneers who settled Marietta.

How to get to Mound Cemetery:

The Mound Cemetery is located at 514 Cutler St. in Marietta, Ohio.

Favorite Places to Camp

The ***Berlin RV Park & Campground*** is lovely, immaculate, and provides an excellent homebase to discover Amish country. I was greeted by a sweet Amish girl in a golf cart. There are laundry facilities, showers, and beautiful campsites. For more information, please visit their website at ***https://www.berlinrv park.com***

Dillon State Park Campground is a large, beautiful campground containing 183 sites, including both tent and RV sites. For more information and to make reservations, please visit https://www.r eserveohio.com

Random Thoughts
What History Means to Me

First, let me start by sharing with you my opinion of what history isn't. History is not a collection of random dates, names, and places for you to memorize. History is not a dry and uninteresting class you have to pass to graduate.

I believe history is a tangible thing. You can actually *feel* history in the places you go, and the sights you see. I remember walking up to the Acropolis in Athens. I looked down at the well-worn marble steps and wondered about how many ancient philosophers had climbed these very steps, thousands of years ago.

You don't have to go far away to experience the *feeling* of history. If you are lucky enough to live in an old house, you may experience history in your own surroundings. You might say to yourself, *"If only these walls could talk."*

During my travels across the United States, I *felt* history in many, many places. If you travel across the country like I did, you will *feel* the wonderful history of our beautiful country for yourself, and you will never be the same. You will discover what it means to be an American.

Why I travel, and why you should too:

I decided to travel across the country by car because I wanted to rediscover America. When I first set out to explore the history of our country, I wanted to find out why America is the greatest country on earth, and what it means to be an American.

The politics of these United States can be frightening and polarizing. I prefer to focus on what unites us, not what divides us. What unites us is we all live in a spectacularly beautiful country, with warm, wonderful people.

I began my journey five years ago, starting out in my Honda CRV. I soon realized I loved the lifestyle, so now I travel in a small RV. From my small RV, I look out on a country with a unique and colorful, multicultural tapestry, unlike any other country on earth.

I have a degree in Archaeology, and a passion for all things archaeological. I love history, with a side love of paleontology. It is these three passions that I set my trip agenda around. I set out to discover the archaeological sites, history, and paleontological world of our country.

As I travel and write my books, I get asked all the time, especially by women, "What is it like to travel by yourself? Aren't you scared?" The truth is, I believe everyone should do what I did. It's a wonderful way to discover our country, and to rediscover yourself. The truth is, I'm scared not to travel. Traveling allows you to get to know yourself, in ways not possible when sitting on the couch watching TV.

We tend to spend a lot of our lives tuning out the world and our place within it. When you travel, you are quite literally forced to deal with your own thoughts, emotions, and feelings. You can discover yourself while traveling. You can come to understand what makes you who you are, and how you can perhaps become a better person. Above all, traveling gives you mental clarity to figure out how to live with intent. It's a way to guide your life, not just wait for things to happen.

Travel Tips & Stuff

What You Need to Know

How to get started:

Planning your trip should be one of the most exciting things about it. You want to be spontaneous, but it is also very wise to plan your route, so you can take full advantage of all the time and miles you will invest.

- First, decide your passions. If you love airplanes, trains, or old vehicles, plan your trip around that. If you love gardens or architecture, seek that out as the focus of your trip.

- Next, read and research areas of the country that will let you enjoy what you are interested in.

- Make a list by state and city or town, of what you want to see.

- Take your handy road atlas and locate the areas on the pages.

- Make a tentative route plan, so you have an idea of where you are going.

Travel tip: Avoid trying to plan your trip down to a schedule of days, hours, or minutes. On a road trip, it will be virtually impossible to know where you will be on any given day. If you adhere to a schedule, you are more likely to stress out, and less likely to actually enjoy yourself, which is the whole point.

What you need:

You need to bring along a sense of adventure and a curious mind. You need to ditch the idea of always being on a schedule, and live a little more spontaneously to thoroughly enjoy yourself. Things will happen as you travel, both good things and bad things, and you need to prepare your mind and your soul for day-to-day changes.

So much of our lives are planned out. Between growing up, going to school, finding a career, marriage, kids, or whatever, people have lost much of the ability to be spontaneous. But you must take spontaneity on the trip with you, because you may make detours along the way to see something really spectacular.

So, for the practical stuff you need:

A great vehicle-I am now five years into the trip and have swapped out my Honda CRV for a small RV, just under 20 feet. I go small because I see humongous RVs on the road, towing a car behind, and all I can think of is, they can't go just anywhere. They are too big. Bad gas mileage, cumbersome to drive, slow, and not agile like my small RV. So, I encourage you, if you want to go car or RV camping and be able to go on remote dirt roads, get an agile vehicle, and small RVs are great.

Travel tip: Don't be afraid to do some modifications to your vehicle. I have made many alterations to my RV, including changing the plumbing, which used to be a mere 4 inches off of the ground, so I would break it all the time. It's now encased in my outside storage compartment. I am also a minimalist, so I have jettisoned anything I won't use or don't love. Don't be afraid to get rid of unnecessary stuff.

An awesome camera that you know inside and out. I use a Nikon and it takes wonderful pictures. Don't skimp on a camera, and don't think a cellphone camera is all you need, because you want the best for your beautiful photos.

Window shades-the best ones are magnetic so you just place them against your windows and they cling to them, obscuring the view inside your car. I also have magnetic window screens, so I can leave my windows down with no bugs!

Battery operated fans and lights-these are important, so you don't have to rely on your house batteries for light and cooling options.

Portable air compressor-this little gem plugs into your cigarette lighter and will inflate your tires if you have a flat. Make sure the air compressor can reach to all of your tires, including your rear tires.

Portable battery charger and power bank-mine comes with battery cables and the power bank, yet once inside the case, it is small enough to put in your glove compartment. This little item, unfortunately, I have had to use, and it saved me.

Portable generator-I have two gas powered generators on the back of my RV, which are hooked together with a coupling unit. I have an interior generator, but after much expense and multiple repairs, it still doesn't work. Now I have generators which will run everything, including AC, and I can maintain them myself.

All season clothing-you never know what different states will bring for weather, so take hot weather and cold weather clothes, and a fair amount of shoes appropriate for hiking, or walking, sandals, and slippers, which are nice at night. Also take along a pair of cheap rubber flip-flops to wear in the public showers you might go into.

Your own pillows-I like my own pillows, so I don't wake up with neck cramps, especially after sleeping in the car.

Sleeping bag and cozy blankets-you want to stay warm and layering is everything.

Warm hat, warm socks, and fuzzy jammies to keep you warm for cold nights sleeping in the car.

A great road atlas, and great guidebooks-get one that's easy to read, with great pictures. For a road atlas, just get one that is easy to read.

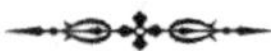

A word about photography:

Along with a great camera, you need to have a great eye. This is easier than it sounds once you have worked with your camera and are comfortable taking pictures with it. I am not a professional photographer, but I like my pictures and other people do too.

These are my tips for taking great pictures:

- Experiment with taking both horizontal and vertical shots.

- Don't always put the subject of the photo in the middle of the photograph.

- This one is important: pay attention to the foreground, and if possible, have something, a plant or whatever, in the foreground to help give the photo dimension and depth.

- This one is important too: turn around often to see the view you just came from. I do this quite often and some of my best pictures have resulted from when I turned around and took the shot.

You can also take a mental photo. Place an image in your mind that you can call upon later. Use all of your senses to see, hear, smell, and maybe even to taste, what is around you. You have the means to fully experience your surroundings, and that is very important to a traveler. When you take a mental photo, be sure to jot down quick little details about what you saw, heard, smelled, or tasted, so you can jog your memory later.

And last, but not least...don't be posing in front of everything, everywhere, to show that you actually went somewhere. Most people want to see themselves in your photo and be mentally transported there, but they can't if you are there already.

To camp or not to camp:

Car or RV camping is great. I prefer it to sleeping on the cold, hard ground in a tent. I can lock the doors, put my window shades up and be cozy for the night.

Some people camp in a Walmart parking lot and feel safe. I do not. I believe that if you are in a busy area, you are more likely to be confronted by a nut job who may bother you. Nothing against Walmart, and many Walmart stores don't allow overnight parking. I don't go for rest areas either because they have a track record of incidents happening to people in rest areas, especially women travelers.

I have come to love casino parking lots. I enjoy gambling, so for a little money, many casinos will provide overnight stays if you gamble a little inside the casino. I also do a lot of boondocking, because it's free, and I believe you are safer parked out in the middle of nowhere in the dark.

I also enjoy camping in state or national campgrounds, wildlife sanctuaries, and fairgrounds.

A word about safety:

When you are a woman traveling alone, it's critical to keep a low profile. Don't tell people you are traveling alone, where you are staying, or any other personal information.

I don't go to bars or get drunk. I'm not preaching but you are on your own, in a city or town you've never been to, and you don't know anyone, so it's not the time to lose control of what you are doing. When you are in control, you are better able to decide which people you want to get to know better.

Travel tip: If you feel vulnerable traveling alone, that's OK. Vulnerability is part of passion, and traveling is a passionate thing to do. You can put one of those family stickers on your vehicle to indicate to others that you are not traveling alone, which can help you feel more secure.

Maintain your connections:

When you are traveling alone, there is a definite sense of disconnection. It feels almost like you are the only one in the world, traveling through space and time. That's why it's critical to keep your connections to loved ones active.

Be on Facebook while you are traveling. You may not have internet a lot of the time, or the internet will be poor. Consider paying to have your phone be a hotspot. It's a little bit of money per month, but it's worth it and has saved me from being without internet. I love the convenience of it, and you will too.

Plan your journey around visiting family members or friends you haven't seen for a long time, or people that are good friends. When you see people you know, it will ground you, so you can continue traveling.

Check in by phone with loved ones. They worry about you, and it's good for both of you to stay connected no matter where you are.

Consider traveling with a pet. I now travel with my 12 year-old sheltie Rosie, after losing my beloved sheltie, Sadie. Rosie is a wonderful companion. She is also an excellent watchdog, and barks her head off at other dogs and people.

Travel tip: One of the easiest and best ways I stay connected while traveling is to offer to take a photo for someone I don't know. Many couples, families, or singles would love to have more pictures of themselves traveling. It's an easy and quick way to have a connection with a fellow traveler, and it's good manners too.

Practical matters:

You need to have an address to send your mail to. Keep in touch with whomever is nice enough to do this for you.

You will also need to come back occasionally to register your car, vote, go to doctor visits, and take care of any other business. You can't leave it all behind, as tempting as that may be.

Bad things that happened:

I have had a few problems, mostly associated with my RV. I bought an older model, vintage 1999, and I have had to do a few repairs.

My worst experience came when I took my rig in to a shop in Spokane, Washington (who shall remain nameless.) All I needed was an oil change. I got the oil change and was about an hour south of town on a Friday at 4:30, when my engine blew.

I was in the middle of the eastern Washington prairie, many miles from the nearest town. All I could do was watch my oil drain out onto the Interstate. I can't help but think it was associated with my oil change, but I couldn't prove it. The moral of this story is: DON'T LET JUST ANYONE WORK ON YOUR VEHICLE.

Good things that happened:

I have met many great people on my travels, from all walks of life. I have also learned not to judge people. I have met numerous homeless people who are often just wanting a kind word, and not to be treated like dirt.

People have mistaken me for a homeless person, and I too, have been treated like dirt. When I can, I try to help people and be kind to them. Most of the time, they smile and reciprocate. You will always meet people who are unkind, but they are just as likely to be driving a huge expensive rig, or to be homeless.

We are all Americans, and we are all part of the human race. When you meet people across the country, you realize just how important it is to get to know your fellow citizens, and learn more about how they view the world and our country.

I have to give a special shout-out to the many dedicated people, often volunteers, who staff our state and national parks and monuments. They work tirelessly to ensure the health of our natural resources, and help travelers enjoy their visit. The same is true of the many people who staff the museums in small towns and large cities. They enjoy history, like I do, and it shows in their smiles.

Along with wonderful people, I have seen an America that is spectacularly beautiful, with open prairies, majestic mountains, and crystal clear rivers. I have seen a small fraction of the history of our country. I have seen the memorials to the brave people who shaped our country. I have fallen in love with America in a way that was not possible sitting in my living room. People ask me, "would I do it again?" The answer comes easily, "Yes, in a heartbeat."

Bibliography & Further Reading

America Revealed, 2012, LIFE Books.

Archaeology of Prophetstown Greenville, Ohio 1805-1808, Richard Green, Tony DeRegnaucourt, Larry Hamilton, Historic Archaeological Research, 1994.

Baron von Steuben, oldfortsteuben.com

Fort Ancient Earthworks & Nature Preserve, hiking & trail guide, Ohio History Connection.

Fort Laurens, Ohio History Connection.

Fort Recovery, Ohio Historical Society.

Guide to the Hopewell Ceremonial Earthworks, World Heritage Ohio, 2019.

Hamtramck, John Francis, *Order in the Wilderness*, oldfortsteuben.com

Haunted Tuscarawas County, Debra Robinson, The History Press, 2016.

Historic Schoenbrunn Village Walking Tour, Ohio History Connection.

Hopewell Ceremonial Earthworks, Hopewellearthworks. org.

Hopewell Culture National Historical Park, National Park Service, 2008.

Marietta Visitor Guide, Marietta Convention and Visitor's Bureau, 2020.

Mound City Group, National Park Service.

National Parks of the Midwest, National Park Service.

Self-Guided Tour of Historic Fort Steuben, oldfortsteuben.com

Silverberg, Robert, *The Mound Builders*, 1970.

The Ghosts of Zoar, Ann Swain and Betty O'Neill-Roderick, Indian River Graphics, Zoar, OH, 2011.

The Mound Cemetery, Marietta Cemeteries Coming Alive.

Traveler's Guide July-December 2021, Ohio History Connection.

Wabash and Fort Recovery Walking Tour, Ohio Humanities.

Welcome to our Museum, Our House Museum brochure, no date

Zoar Village, Ohio History Connection.

Index

Referenced by Sections

B

C

D

E

M

N

O

Tomb of the Unknown Patriot of the American Revolution-see Fort Laurens

Treaty of Greenville-see Fort Recovery

U

Uncle Tom's Cabin-see John Rankin House

Underground Railroad-see John Rankin House

V

Valley Forge-see Fort Steuben

Voices from the past-see Fort Recovery, Fort Laurens, John Rankin House, Campus Martius Museum, Fort Steuben

Von Steuben, Baron Friedrich Wilhelm-see Fort Steuben

W

Washington, George-see Fort Steuben

Wayne, General Anthony-see Fort Recovery

Whipple, Abraham-see Mound Cemetery

Woodland tradition-see Fort Ancient Earthworks

Wurttemberg-see Zoar Village

Z

Zeisberger, David-see Schoenbrunn Village

About the Author

Julie Bettendorf is a world traveler with a degree in archaeology and a background in history. She has traveled extensively throughout Egypt, Central America, South America, Europe, and the United Kingdom, visiting archaeological and historical sites all along the way.

Currently, Julie is traveling around the US visiting ghost towns, ancient rock art sites, and archaeological wonders as part of research for her ongoing historical travel series entitled *Wandering Woman*. Wandering Woman is a set of state-by-state guides, full of photographs, historical anecdotes, and unique tips to help other women travel and explore solo across the US by car or RV. Julie enjoys writing freelance blogs, traveling frequently with her two adult children, and hiking outdoors with her faithful dog companion Rosie.

Also By Julie Bettendorf

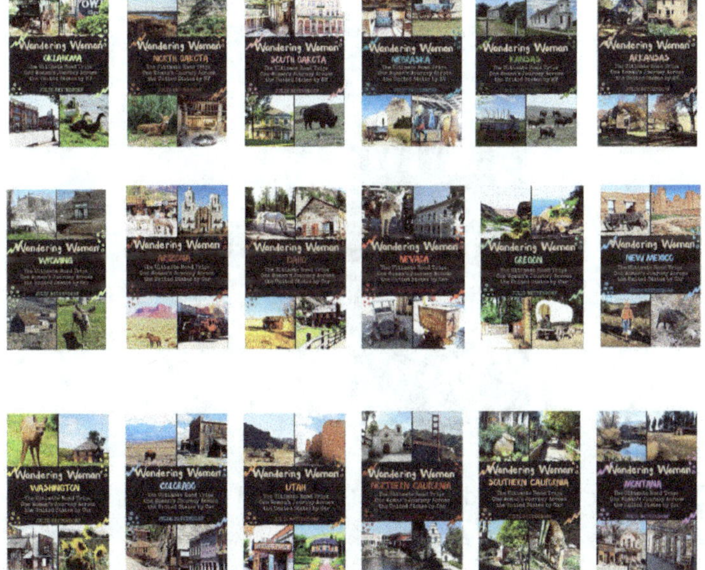

Wandering Woman: Ohio is the most recent book in the *Wandering Woman Travel Series*. Additional books in the *Wandering Woman: Travel Series are* available in ebook and paperback.

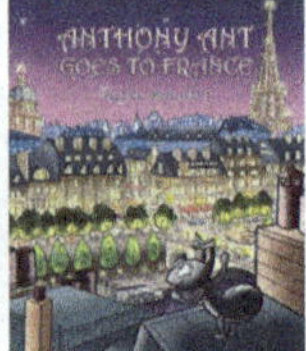

Julie has published two children's books in an ongoing, beautifully illustrated travel series entitled *Anthony Ant Goes to France* and *Anthony Ant Goes to Egypt*.

She has also published a work of historical fiction entitled *Luxor: Book of Past Lives* which has recently been released as an audiobook, read by renowned narrator Barry Shannon.

CRISTO

É

TUDO

H.G. Souza

S729 Souza, H.G.
    Cristo é tudo : o mistério da vontade de Deus é de
  fazer convergir em Cristo todas as coisas / H.G. Souza. —
  1. ed. — Goiânia : H.G. Souza, 2026.
    140 p. ; 23 cm.

    ISBN 979-8-9946034-2-0

    1. Vida e prática cristã. 2. Cristianismo - Doutrinas.
  3. Jesus Cristo - Ensinamentos. 4. Fé. 5. Crescimento
  espiritual. 6. Literatura devocional. I. Título.

                  CDD23: 248.4

F-1003261

Bibliotecária: Priscila Pena Machado - CRB-7/6971

Sumário

Endosso

Cristo é Tudo é um livro que te capacita a entrar em um realinhamento de visão, identidade e esperança. Este não é um convite para um Cristianismo com base em esforços; é um convite para você enxergar mais claramente Aquele que já sustém toda a sua vida. Helber traz uma mensagem simples, mas que transforma vidas: Deus tem um único plano para sua vida, uma única fonte para o seu crescimento, e uma única resposta para toda e qualquer necessidade — e o nome d'Ele é Jesus. Este livro te chama profeticamente de volta à verdade de que Cristo não é apenas o seu Salvador — Ele é a sua vida.

Enquanto você lê, espere que o Espírito Santo tire seus olhos do que você pensa que te falta e te ancore naquilo que você já tem. Paciência, humildade, amor e poder não são metas distantes que você precisa alcançar; são o fruto natural de permanecer em Cristo. A cruz não é meramente um evento passado — é uma realidade presente que declara que sua identidade está segura, seu futuro está resolvido, e sua transformação é inevitável. Este livro libera esperança em sua vida porque remove a pressão. Ele te lembra que o crescimento não vem do esforço próprio, mas de uma união; não de se consertar a si mesmo, mas de confiar na obra consumada de Jesus. Você não está perdendo algo — você está descobrindo Alguém. E à medida que Cristo se revela mais plenamente a você, a liberdade virá naturalmente.

Eu creio que Cristo é Tudo despertará alegria, restaurará a confiança e renovará a visão em seu coração. Que este livro fortaleça a sua fé, traga descanso de suas tentativas e te leve a declarar para si mesmo: "Os melhores dias da minha vida estão por vir!"

Steve Backlund - Igniting Hope Ministries

Introdução

Deixe-me compartilhar um pouco sobre como Deus entrou na minha vida para uma longa caminhada, e não apenas para momentos passageiros. Fui criado em uma família cristã, era o que dizíamos. No começo minha vida cristã se baseava em uma rotina de infância. Minhas primeiras lembranças dela envolvem ir à missa com minha mãe todo domingo às 7h da manhã, seguido por uma visita à feira para a compra da semana. Por anos, essa foi a programação das manhãs de domingo. Meu entendimento de Deus se limitava à mensagem de que Ele enviou Jesus, Seu Filho, para nos salvar. O conceito de ser 'salvo', porém, permanecia indefinido.

Por volta dos dez anos, observei um papel diferente para Deus. Minha mãe se referia a Ele como a solução para problemas que pareciam não ter uma resposta prática. Durante esse período, a fé dos meus pais parecia real, mas privada, expressa através de orações, no silêncio do seu quarto, para um Deus aparentemente distante. A regularidade da nossa presença na missa dominical diminuiu, e eu só ouvia o nome de Deus ser mencionado com reverência pelos meus pais. O ritual de fé que estava estabelecido começou então a diminuir.

Veio a adolescência e, aos quinze anos, introduziu a ideia de Deus como um último recurso em momentos de dificuldade. Eu trabalhando fora, estudando a noite, novas amizades e com mudanças na aparência, o que não era por rebeldia, mas por uma busca de identidade, tudo isso causou uma mudança notável em mim. Meu pai nessa época decidiu por uma intervenção, comprou uma Bíblia e propôs que a lêssemos juntos. Antes disso, eu não me recordo de alguma vez ter interagido com uma Bíblia física.

A experiência inicial de ler a Bíblia com meu pai foi desafiadora. Lemos apenas algumas páginas, e nenhum de nós parecia entender o contexto completo. Senti uma clara resistência àquela prática. No entanto, observei que meu pai continuou a ler independentemente de mim. Essa tentativa compartilhada de leitura da Bíblia, combinada com a memória anterior das orações privadas da minha mãe, estabeleceu um senso fundamental em mim: a observação de que Deus era real e não tão distante quanto eu pensava, uma presença que existia independentemente da minha capacidade de percebê-Lo ou compreendê-Lo.

Essa percepção culminou aos dezoito anos: concluí nessa época que Deus estava em uma busca, estava à minha busca. Isso não foi uma resposta a uma crise existencial ou coisa assim; no fundo, eu estava desesperado por Jesus e não sabia. Minha real vida cristã começou com esse reconhecimento da Sua presença. Comecei a ver que Ele tinha estado consistentemente presente, independente do que eu cria, esperando que eu O reconhecesse, esperando que eu abraçasse Sua obra na cruz.

A principal conclusão que tirei foi esta: Deus está comigo para uma longa jornada, não apenas para um conserto de caráter momentâneo. A obra da cruz na minha vida não é um evento histórico, é um evento diário. O plano de Deus para mim é convergir "todas as coisas" em Cristo, e eu quero dizer "tudo mesmo", quer eu entenda ou não. Isso também não é um evento histórico da minha adolescência, mas é a Sua obra diária em mim. Para mim, não há vida cristã separada de Cristo e da obra contínua da cruz.

É na cruz que Cristo diz "Está consumado" (João 19:30), e é lá, onde Ele diz que está consumado, que minha vida real começa e tem fim.

1

Nada Além de Cristo

Se você escolheu ler este livro, é porque, sabendo ou não, você tem um desejo profundo por Cristo. E a boa notícia é que, sabendo ou não, Cristo também tem um desejo profundo por você. Deus Pai tem um plano único para a vida, para qualquer tipo de vida, e o plano Dele é o Filho. Parece simplista, mas sim, é simples assim. O mistério da vontade de Deus é de fazer convergir em Cristo "todas as coisas".

A vida cristã, como o nome sugere, é uma vida em Cristo. Vejamos como Romanos 11:36 explica a dinâmica da vida cristã: "Porque dele, e por meio dele, e para ele são todas as coisas". Portanto, é bem simples: para nós, a vida vem de Cristo, nós a vivemos por meio de Cristo, e nosso maior objetivo na vida também é o próprio Cristo.

O mistério da vontade de Deus é de fazer convergir em Cristo todas as coisas (Efésios 1:9-10, ARA).

Nossa Segurança, Nossa Fonte, Nosso Tudo

Jesus lhes disse: "Quando levantardes o Filho do homem, então sabereis quem eu sou." (João 8:28, ARA). Esta é uma promessa profunda e encorajadora! Jesus está nos revelando que Seu sacrifício supremo — Sua obra voluntária na cruz, o momento em que Ele foi 'levantado' — é a chave para a mais profunda revelação de Sua verdadeira identidade. Quando olhamos para a cruz, não vemos apenas um evento histórico; vemos o próprio coração de amor e da graça salvadora de Deus. Naquele momento glorioso, descobrimos a verdade completa de que Ele é, de fato, nosso Salvador, nosso Senhor e a resposta para toda e qualquer necessidade.

A maravilhosa verdade é que você já morreu para a sua velha vida, e a sua nova e real vida está escondida em segurança com Cristo em Deus. (Romanos 6:4-8). E quando "Cristo, que é a nossa vida, se manifestar, então também vós vos manifestareis com ele em glória." (Colossenses 3:3-4).

A maravilhosa verdade é que você já morreu para a sua velha vida, e a sua vida nova e real está escondida em segurança com Cristo em Deus. E quando Cristo, que é a nossa vida, se manifestar, então também vós vos manifestareis com ele em glória!

Que segurança e futuro incríveis nós temos! Isso não é apenas uma promessa distante; é uma realidade profunda e presente. Por você estar unido a Cristo, seu verdadeiro eu é intocável, escondido no lugar mais seguro do universo. Agora mesmo, Cristo *é* a sua vida — a própria fonte de sua força, alegria e propósito. Um dia, quando Ele brilhar em Sua glória completa, você brilhará junto com Ele! Até lá, viva cada dia com confiança, sabendo que sua identidade está segura e selada Nele.

Pense nesta verdade magnífica: Tudo — absolutamente tudo — foi criado nele, por meio dele e para ele. O apóstolo Paulo afirma: "Porque nele foram criadas todas as coisas que há nos céus e na terra, visíveis e invisíveis, sejam tronos, sejam dominações, sejam principados, sejam potestades; tudo foi criado por ele e para ele. E ele é antes de todas as coisas, e todas as coisas subsistem por ele. E ele é a cabeça do corpo, da igreja; é o princípio e o primogênito dentre os mortos, para que em tudo tenha a preeminência. Porque foi do agrado do Pai que toda a plenitude nele habitasse, E que, havendo por ele feito a paz pelo sangue da sua cruz, por meio dele reconciliasse consigo mesmo todas as coisas, tanto as que estão na terra, como as que estão nos céus." (Colossenses 1:16-20).

Essa passagem pinta o retrato mais deslumbrante de Jesus Cristo! Isso significa que Ele não é apenas uma parte da sua vida; Ele é o projeto divino para toda a vida, a "força" que impede o seu mundo de se desfazer e o propósito máximo de toda a criação. Essa verdade nos empodera e capacita! Você está conectado Àquele que é a fonte de todo o poder, toda a glória e toda a vida. Por causa da Sua obra consumada na cruz, o conflito entre Deus e a humanidade acabou, e você está reconciliado com Deus, vivendo em um estado de paz eterna. Ele é o *Tudo em Todos*, e você está maravilhosamente enxertado *Nele*.

O Dom Transformador: Uma Única Coisa é Necessária

A magnífica, e única provisão que recebemos de Deus é Seu Filho, Jesus Cristo. No entanto, como crentes, nosso entendimento dessa verdade importantíssima varia drasticamente. Alguns veem Jesus como uma dádiva, uma benção importante entre uma vasta coleção de outras bênçãos espirituais, enquanto outros compreenderam a gloriosa realidade de que Ele é o *único* dom de Deus que abrange tudo. Podemos, inicialmente, receber Cristo como uma dádiva — Aquele que nos salva — mas assumimos erroneamente que milhares de outros dons e virtudes, de menor importância, devem ser adquiridos separadamente ao longo do tempo. Uma confissão mais profunda, no entanto, é que Jesus Cristo não é apenas *uma* dádiva; Ele é *tudo*, a única provisão de Deus para cada aspecto de nossas vidas. Essa profunda diferença de perspectiva é a chave para destravar uma vida cristã verdadeiramente vitoriosa, uma vida de descanso.

Pode ser surpreendente quando começamos nossa jornada com Cristo e logo descobrimos que ser "salvo" não apaga instantaneamente todos os nossos defeitos e lutas. Podemos perceber que um temperamento explosivo e frustrante ainda se manifesta, o orgulho ainda direciona sutilmente nossas decisões, ou que uma velha e paralisante falta de esperança ainda aperta nossos corações. Tornamo-nos novos cristãos, sim, mas somos novos cristãos com deficiências de caráter notáveis. Nossa resposta natural e imediata a essas imperfeições é lutar para corrigi-las.

Neste estágio da experiência cristã, é comum nos encontrarmos orando, esperando e buscando diligentemente inúmeros "dons" individuais para preencher essas lacunas que foram percebidas. Oramos sinceramente por paciência, pedimos por humildade e tentamos desesperadamente cultivar mais amor. Naturalmente, contamos Cristo entre esses dons — o mais importante, é claro — mas ainda assim apenas mais um item em uma longa lista de compras espirituais. Quando sentimos que superamos com sucesso uma deficiência específica — finalmente controlando o temperamento ou vencendo o orgulho — nosso coração se alegra genuinamente com o que percebemos ser uma aquisição bem-sucedida, uma nova "dádiva" obtida da mão de Deus.

A Mentalidade de "Adicionar" ao que Nos Falta

Com este entendimento comum, mas incompleto, muitos crentes veem a graça de Deus como um "kit de reparo" espiritual — um suprimento divino projetado apenas para repor suas carências ou "desejos" individuais. Nessa mentalidade, a vida cristã se torna uma espécie de preencher o que está faltando. Podemos pensar: "Para que mais serve a graça de Deus, senão para preencher as qualidades que me faltam?" Nos vemos como fundamentalmente bons, e apenas nos faltam alguns itens para a perfeição. "Meu amor é quase perfeito", pode pensar alguém, "mas seria ainda melhor se eu pudesse apenas adicionar um pouco de humildade e uma pitada de paciência. Uma vez adicionados esses suplementos, então estarei completo, serei um cristão maduro." Esse conceito humano está profundamente enraizado em nosso senso de falta e, como resultado, estamos constantemente pedindo a Deus por suprimentos específicos e notórios que acreditamos precisar.

Encaramos nossos pedidos por essas virtudes como "coisas" ou "objetos" distintos que nos faltam. Olhamos para os outros, medindo nossas necessidades contra o que aparentemente eles têm: "Eu gostaria de não ser tão impaciente; olhe como o Senhor Fulano de Tal é paciente! Eu gostaria de não ser tão orgulhoso; olhe como aquela mulher é gentil e humilde." É incrivelmente difícil orar por algo que ainda não vimos, então muitas vezes acabamos orando por uma medida de humildade ou paciência que se assemelha ao que outra pessoa exibe. Este foco externo em uma característica visível que outra pessoa possui é a essência do problema.

Tudo o que é bom, verdadeiro e de valor flui apenas de Cristo. A jornada cristã não é uma busca por uma coleção de traços espirituais; é um aprofundamento, um relacionamento íntimo com a Única Pessoa em quem todas as virtudes residem perfeitamente.

Imagine isto: se Deus pegasse agora a paciência de outra pessoa e a "depositasse" em você, você ficaria satisfeito? Muito provavelmente, sua resposta seria um alegre *sim*! Esse desejo profundo decorre do fato de que frequentemente vemos virtudes espirituais — como a paciência — como uma *coisa* separada e mensurável que outros possuem e que nós, infelizmente, não temos. Podemos lutar contra uma profunda autocrítica, odiando-nos pelo nosso temperamento e desejando que pudéssemos simplesmente adquirir essa virtude. Consequentemente, muitos na igreja anseiam por um item específico — um temperamento controlado, um espírito quieto — que acreditam ser uma virtude que Deus possui e concedeu a certas pessoas espirituais, mas que ainda lhes falta. A necessidade urgente deles, como a veem, é simplesmente ter essa "coisa" adicionada a eles para que também possam ser pessoas pacientes e completas.

A Diferença: Cristo versus Conceitos

Este é o ponto de divergência entre um Cristianismo vibrante, vivo e autêntico e um que é falho ou meramente teórico. Muitos crentes sinceros estão constantemente procurando por algo — uma virtude, um traço, uma qualidade espiritual — que parece estar em toda parte, exceto em suas próprias vidas. Eles observam isso em outras pessoas, mas não o possuem. Assim, todo o seu foco espiritual se torna uma busca por uma 'coisa' avulsa e tangível que podem buscar, possuir e depois celebrar quando é adquirida. Eles buscam aquele 'item', obtêm o 'item' e se alegram com o 'item' adquirido.

A gloriosa e libertadora verdade que o Espírito Santo quer nos revelar é esta: No reino de Deus, não há "coisa" separada de Cristo. Não existe um item separado chamado "paciência", ou "humildade", ou "luz" que exista de forma independente. Há somente Cristo, e só Ele.

Tudo o que é bom, verdadeiro e de valor flui apenas da pessoa de Jesus. A jornada cristã não é uma busca por uma coleção de traços espirituais; é um aprofundamento, um relacionamento íntimo com a Única Pessoa em quem todas as virtudes residem perfeitamente. É uma mudança de se esforçar para *ter* uma coisa para simplesmente *permanecer* na Pessoa.

Pai Celeste, chegamos diante de Ti com corações cheios de gratidão pelo profundo mistério e simplicidade da Tua vontade de convergir todas as coisas em Cristo.

Obrigado pela gloriosa verdade de que Cristo não é apenas uma dádiva, mas o Sua dádiva *única* e *completa* — a provisão total para cada aspecto de nossas vidas. Somos gratos porque nossa jornada não é um esforço para adquirir virtudes, mas um relacionamento íntimo e de descanso com a Pessoa viva de Jesus Cristo, em quem todas as virtudes residem perfeitamente.

Nós Te agradecemos, Senhor, porque no Seu reino não existe uma "coisa" separada de Cristo. Nós Te louvamos porque a nossa velha vida está verdadeiramente morta, e a nossa nova e real vida está escondida em segurança com Cristo em Deus. Que segurança e futuro incríveis nós temos!

Pai, que possamos viver cada dia com confiança, descansando na verdade libertadora de que Cristo é a nossa vida, a nossa fonte e o nosso tudo. Que o nosso foco seja firmado não em uma mentalidade religiosa, mas sim em simplesmente permanecer Nele, o nosso Tudo em Todos.

Amém.

2

Cristo é o Tudo de Deus

"No dia seguinte João viu a Jesus, que vinha para ele, e disse: Eis o Cordeiro de Deus, que tira o pecado do mundo." (Jo 1:29)

"E Jesus lhes disse: Eu sou o pão da vida; aquele que vem a mim não terá fome, e quem crê em mim nunca terá sede." (Jo 6:35)

"Disse-lhes, pois, Jesus: Na verdade, na verdade vos digo que, se não comerdes a carne do Filho do homem, e não beberdes o seu sangue, não tereis vida em vós mesmos." (Jo 6:53)

"Falou-lhes, pois, Jesus outra vez, dizendo: Eu sou a luz do mundo; quem me segue não andará em trevas, mas terá a luz da vida." (Jo 8:12)

"Por isso vos disse que morrereis em vossos pecados; porque, se não crerdes que eu sou, morrereis em vossos pecados." (Jo 8:24)

"Disse-lhes, pois, Jesus: Quando levantardes o Filho do homem, então sabereis quem eu sou, e que nada faço por mim mesmo; mas isto falo como meu Pai me ensinou." (Jo 8:28)

"Disse-lhe Jesus: Eu sou a ressurreição e a vida; quem crê em mim, ainda que esteja morto, viverá;" (Jo 11:25)

"Disse-lhe Jesus: Eu sou o caminho, e a verdade e a vida; ninguém vem ao Pai, senão por mim." (Jo 14:6)

"Mas vós sois dele, em Jesus Cristo, o qual para nós foi feito por Deus sabedoria, e justiça, e santificação, e redenção;" (1 Co 1:30)

"Quando Cristo, que é a nossa vida, se manifestar, então também vós vos manifestareis com ele em glória." (Cl 3:4)

"Paulo, apóstolo de Jesus Cristo, segundo o mandado de Deus, nosso Salvador, e do Senhor Jesus Cristo, esperança nossa," (1 Tm 1:1)

"O SENHOR é a minha luz e a minha salvação; a quem temerei? O SENHOR é a força da minha vida; de quem me recearei?" (Sl 27:1)

Cristo: Tanto o Propósito Divino para Nós Quanto a Nossa Jornada até Ele

No grandioso tecer do plano eterno de Deus, Cristo se apresenta tanto como o destino final quanto o próprio caminho que nos conduz a ele. É uma jornada linda que começa em Cristo, acontece por meio de Cristo e culmina em Cristo. Para compreendermos de verdade a profundidade do magnífico propósito de Deus, podemos recorrer aos profundos ensinamentos encontrados nos livros de Efésios e Colossenses, que iluminam essa verdade divina.

Efésios revela de forma maravilhosa como, de acordo com o plano intencional e amoroso de Deus, Ele orquestrou toda a história para convergir e encontrar seu glorioso cumprimento em Cristo. Imagine uma sinfonia cósmica onde cada nota, cada instrumento, cada movimento, está perfeitamente harmonizado para trazer tudo — tanto nos céus quanto na terra — a uma magnífica unidade centrada em Jesus. É uma visão impressionante de toda a criação encontrando Nele seu verdadeiro sentido e propósito.

Colossenses leva essa revelação ainda mais adiante, mostrando-nos que Cristo não é apenas uma figura central, mas que Ele é absolutamente preeminente em todos os aspectos da existência. E mais do que isso, Ele deve ser o tudo e estar em todos. Isso significa que Cristo não é meramente o objetivo pelo qual estamos lutando; Ele é também o próprio poder, a própria presença e essência que nos capacita a alcançar esse objetivo. Ele é o meio pelo qual o grandioso projeto de Deus se desenrola. O desejo mais profundo de Deus é que Cristo ocupe a posição suprema em tudo. Para isso, Cristo deve ser tudo.

É apenas através de Sua natureza que tudo abrange, e de Sua presença em todas as coisas, que Ele pode verdadeiramente unir tudo — tanto celestial quanto terrestre — em perfeito alinhamento. Se Cristo é verdadeiramente tudo, então é uma consequência natural que todas as coisas encontrem Nele a sua plenitude. Se Ele vive e dá vida a tudo, o que mais poderia definir a existência?

Cristo é absolutamente preeminente em todos os aspectos da existência. Mais do que isso, Ele deve ser o tudo e estar em todos. Isso significa que Cristo não é meramente o objetivo pelo qual estamos lutando; Ele é também o próprio poder, a própria presença e a própria essência que nos capacita a alcançar esse objetivo.

É uma verdade libertadora lembrar que, aos olhos de Deus, existe apenas Cristo, e não uma infinidade de "coisas" ou "dádivas" separadas. Ele não vê eventos isolados ou questões desconexas; Seu olhar está unicamente fixado em Cristo. As complexidades e preocupações que frequentemente preenchem nossas mentes humanas — a interminável "lista de coisas" que percebemos no mundo hoje — são, da perspectiva eterna de Deus, simplesmente inexistentes à parte de Cristo. Nosso ponto de vista mundano pode categorizar incontáveis problemas e questões, mas de acordo com a sabedoria infinita de Deus, Cristo é onipresente. Consequentemente, não existem dádivas ou coisas verdadeiramente separadas dele; Cristo é tudo, e Ele está em todos. E essa realidade gloriosa é precisamente quando o propósito eterno de Deus será pleno e magnificamente realizado.

Abrace esta verdade incrível: Cristo, com amor e poder, trará todas as coisas à perfeita unidade consigo mesmo. Esta não é uma esperança futura e distante; é uma obra linda que já começou e está se desenrolando ativamente na igreja hoje. Não é algo que só começará em uma era futura, nem só se tornará verdade quando o propósito eterno de Deus atingir sua culminação final.

Deus, em Sua graça sem limites, está ativamente abrindo nossos olhos espirituais agora mesmo para vermos que, dentro da igreja, Cristo é tanto a própria essência de nossos esforços espirituais quanto a substância de todas as verdadeiras realidades espirituais. A igreja está começando a despertar para essa compreensão profunda, e ao fazermos isso, começamos a viver este mundo espiritual vibrante. Se a igreja continua a perceber uma separação entre "coisas" e "dádivas" e Cristo, isso simplesmente indica que ainda não compreendemos totalmente a gloriosa visão de Cristo como o tudo. E, é claro, as "coisas" e as "dádivas" de que falamos aqui não são apenas para as questões diárias deste mundo; elas apontam especialmente para as profundas questões espirituais e divinas que verdadeiramente definem nossa existência Nele.

É bastante notável como o Evangelho de João inclui tantas percepções e narrativas únicas que não são encontradas nos outros relatos bíblicos da vida de Jesus. Este Evangelho, considerado o mais profundo e o último a ser escrito entre eles, surgiu após todo o Novo Testamento já ter tomado forma, seguindo os outros Evangelhos e inúmeras Epístolas. A contribuição de João, portanto, serve como uma revelação culminante, oferecendo-nos um vislumbre profundo da avaliação final de Deus sobre Cristo e nos guiando sobre como nós também podemos chegar a conhecer Cristo da mesma maneira íntima que Deus O conhece.

Através da escrita inspirada de João, chegamos a uma compreensão mais profunda de que o desejo final de Deus não é meramente um cordeiro sacrificial, nem que Ele simplesmente fornece "o pão da vida" como uma dádiva externa. Aprendemos também que Deus não apenas *fornece* o caminho, a verdade e a vida como conceitos separados, nem que Cristo simplesmente *usa* Seu poder para restaurar a vida ou a visão humana. Pelo contrário, a verdade avassaladora e singular tecida em todo o Evangelho de João é que Cristo é todas essas coisas.

Deus, em Sua graça sem limites, está ativamente abrindo nossos olhos espirituais agora mesmo para vermos que, dentro da igreja, Cristo é tanto a própria essência de nossos esforços espirituais quanto a substância de todas as verdadeiras realidades espirituais.

Quando Jesus declara: "Eu sou a luz do mundo", Ele não está dizendo que *pode dar* luz às pessoas; Ele está afirmando que *é* a própria fonte e essência da luz em si. Da mesma forma, quando Ele afirma: "Eu sou o pão da vida", Ele não está prometendo *nos fornecer* pão; Ele está proclamando que *é* o sustento vital que nossas almas realmente anseiam. Ele diz: "Eu sou o caminho", e não que Ele *nos guiará* por um caminho. Ele proclama: "Eu sou a verdade", e não que Ele *nos ensinará* uma verdade. E Ele afirma: "Eu sou a vida verdadeira", e não que Ele *nos concederá* uma vida. Essa profunda distinção é poderosamente ilustrada quando Lázaro morreu: Cristo não disse a Maria e Marta que *tinha o poder* de ressuscitar o irmão delas; em vez disso, Ele declarou: "Eu sou a ressurreição". Ele não é apenas Aquele que *faz* essas coisas; Ele *é* a própria personificação delas.

É crucial entender este princípio fundamental: no Cristianismo, não existem meras "coisas" ou conceitos abstratos separados de Cristo. O "pão da vida", a "luz", o "caminho", a "verdade", a "própria vida", a "ressurreição", ou mesmo "o cordeiro" – estas não são entidades independentes. Não, o cerne da questão é que existe *somente Cristo*! O que nós realmente precisamos compreender em nossa caminhada com Deus é que nossa experiência espiritual não é sobre adquirir uma lista de "coisas" espirituais ou se engajar em uma busca por "dádivas". É unicamente sobre o próprio Cristo. Não é que Ele nos *dá* luz, mas que Ele *é* a nossa luz. Não é que Ele *lidera* o caminho, mas Ele *é* o caminho. Não é que Ele *nos concede* uma vida, mas Ele *é* a nossa vida. Não é que Ele ensina uma verdade, mas Ele *é* a verdade. Você percebe a profunda diferença aqui? Cada coisa que Cristo dá é, na verdade, Seu próprio Ser, estendido a nós em amor e graça.

Descobrindo o Cristo do Evangelho de João

É realmente fascinante ver como o Evangelho de João se destaca dos demais. Não foi apenas outro relato histórico; foi escrito por último, oferecendo uma perspectiva espiritual profunda que complementa de forma linda a narrativa do Novo Testamento. O texto de João é profundamente focado, indo além do ministério diário para nos mostrar a visão definitiva de Deus sobre Seu Filho — e como nós também podemos chegar a conhecer Cristo da maneira mais íntima e transformadora. É um convite para irmos de crer simplesmente a um encontro radical e transformador.

O que descobrimos na mensagem de João é uma poderosa mudança de perspectiva. Ela desafia a ideia tradicional de que Deus simplesmente nos fornece itens ou serviços espirituais para usarmos. Não é que Deus nos oferece um cordeiro sacrificial em abstrato, ou nos entrega um pedaço de "pão da vida", ou nos dá um mapa espiritual a seguir. João deixa bem claro: Jesus não apenas usa Seu poder para dar vida, luz ou verdade; Ele é a própria essência de todas essas coisas.

Essa percepção é o fato monumental e central do Evangelho de João: Cristo é a realidade que abrange e que sustenta toda a nossa fé. Quando Ele diz: "Eu sou a luz do mundo", Ele não está dizendo: "Eu sou capaz de lhes dar luz." Quando Ele declara: "Eu sou o pão da vida", Ele não está prometendo apenas fornecer alimento espiritual. Ele não oferece nos guiar ao Caminho; Ele é o Caminho que trilhamos. Ele não nos ensina uma verdade; Ele é a corporificação viva de toda a Verdade. E diante da morte, Ele não apenas garantiu a Maria e Marta: "Eu tenho o poder de ressuscitar o irmão de vocês." Em vez disso, na mais profunda declaração de Seu próprio ser, Ele disse: "Eu sou a ressurreição."

Esta é uma verdade imensamente libertadora para nós hoje: No Cristianismo, o foco nunca está em "coisas" externas, mas unicamente na Pessoa viva de Cristo!

O evangelho de João deixa bem claro: Jesus não apenas usa Seu poder para dar vida, luz ou verdade; Ele é a essência de todas essas coisas.

Pense nas "coisas" que muitas vezes buscamos: luz, orientação, vida no espírito, verdade, poder, ressurreição. Esses são conceitos maravilhosos, mas o ponto principal é este: em nossa experiência real com Deus, não recebemos meras coisas ou dádivas religiosas; recebemos o próprio Cristo. Não é que Ele nos dá luz, mas que Ele é a nossa Luz que brilha de dentro. Não é que Ele lidera o caminho, mas que Ele é o Caminho em que habitamos. Não é que Ele nos entrega uma vida, mas que Ele é a nossa própria Fonte de Vida! Ele não simplesmente nos ensina a verdade; Ele é a Verdade que nos liberta.

Você percebe a incrível diferença aqui? Este não é apenas um ponto teológico sutil; é a chave para uma vida espiritual florescente e sem esforço! Tudo o que Cristo dá é o Seu próprio ser — Seu amor, Sua natureza, Sua vitória, Sua paz.

A boa notícia é que o plano de Deus para sua vida é maravilhosamente simples: Cristo é o tudo de Deus, porque Deus não lhe oferece nada menos que Seu Filho! Ele não lhe deu um conjunto de regras ou uma lista fragmentada de bênçãos; Ele lhe deu Cristo. Ele dá Cristo para ser a sua luz, Cristo para ser a sua força, Cristo para ser o seu sustento diário, e Cristo para ser o glorioso Caminho, a Verdade duradoura e a Vida abundante.

Quando seus olhos são abertos para este fato glorioso, a pressão para fazer mais, alcançar mais, ou lembrar um método complexo se dissolve. Sua jornada espiritual é transformada de um esforço por um produto religioso em simplesmente receber e desfrutar de um relacionamento com a Pessoa que é tudo o que você sempre precisará. Olhe para Ele hoje, pois em Cristo, você tem todas as coisas.

Como Paulo e Davi viram o Cristo

Quero que você compreenda a grande verdade que o apóstolo Paulo entendeu profundamente — uma verdade que se alinha perfeitamente com o que o próprio Jesus declarou. Paulo conhecia o Senhor intimamente, e suas cartas revelam fatos profundos e transformadores sobre o que Cristo significa para nós.

Cristo É a Nossa Esperança - Primeiramente, Paulo diz a Timóteo que "Cristo Jesus (é) a nossa esperança" (1 Timóteo 1:1). Essa frase não ressoa com poder? É muito mais libertador do que dizer: "Nossa esperança está em Cristo." Essa pequena palavra "em" pode implicar que estamos depositando uma expectativa em uma figura externa, esperando que Ele nos dê esperança. Mas Paulo diz que Cristo Jesus é a esperança. Ele é a realidade viva, pulsante e inabalável do nosso futuro, da nossa segurança e da nossa expectativa confiante. Não é uma coisa que Ele nos dá para nos apegarmos; é Ele mesmo habitando em você como a garantia absoluta da glória. Sua esperança não é um sentimento que se esvai; é uma Pessoa que nunca falha.

Cristo É a Nossa Vida - Então, em sua carta aos Colossenses, Paulo nos entrega outra obra-prima: "Quando Cristo, que é a nossa vida, se manifestar" (Colossenses 3:4). Observe a simplicidade profunda: "Cristo, que é a nossa vida." Ele não diz: "Quando a vida que Cristo dá for revelada", mas sim, "Quando Cristo, a nossa vida, for revelado". Isso muda o jogo espiritual! Isso nos força a ver que a totalidade da vida cristã não é sobre adquirir bênçãos ou atributos espirituais, mas sobre possuir uma Pessoa. De fato, um cristão não possui nada além de Cristo — e Nele, temos tudo. Ele não é apenas o que dá vida abundante;

Ele é a fonte divina e espontânea de vida fluindo através de você a cada momento.

Cristo É a Nossa Sabedoria, Justiça, Santificação e Redenção - Talvez uma das escrituras mais encorajadoras e centrais seja 1 Coríntios 1:30, onde Paulo declara que Deus nos colocou em Cristo Jesus, o qual se tornou para nós, da parte de Deus, sabedoria, e justiça, e santificação, e redenção. Este versículo poderoso revela o coração do plano de Deus. Deus não nos entregou "dádivas" ou "coisas" separadas e individuais:

- Ele não nos deu apenas justiça; Ele nos dá Cristo, que é a nossa Justiça.
- Ele não nos deu simplesmente um processo de santificação; Ele nos dá Cristo, que é a nossa própria Santificação.
- Ele não nos deu meramente um ato externo de redenção; Ele nos dá Cristo, que é a nossa Redenção.
- Ele não nos deu simplesmente conhecimento; Ele nos dá Cristo, que é a nossa Sabedoria.

É por isso que podemos proclamar com ousadia que o Cristo de Deus é o tudo de Deus. Além d'Ele, Deus não oferece nenhum outro "pacote" espiritual.

Tomemos, por exemplo, a nossa justificação. Paulo não diz que Deus fez de Jesus o nosso "justificador" (embora Ele seja isso também!). Ele diz que Deus fez de Jesus a nossa justificação. Isso é muito mais do que uma declaração legal; é uma realidade pessoal. Jesus não veio para nos santificar e depois nos deixar com a tarefa para mantê-la; Ele veio para ser a nossa

Santificação — uma obra viva, constante e sem esforço. Nossa santificação não é um comportamento, um conjunto de ações ou um dever religioso; é uma Pessoa, o próprio Cristo, sendo vivido através de nós.

Esta verdade linda e vital permanece: Cristo não é apenas o nosso Redentor, mas também a nossa Redenção. Ele não é apenas o nosso Santificador, mas também a nossa Santificação. Ele não é apenas o nosso Justificador, mas também a nossa Justiça. Ele não é apenas Aquele que nos torna sábios, mas Ele mesmo é a nossa Sabedoria.

Graças a Deus por esta mensagem libertadora! Quando você compreende de verdade que Cristo lhe dá a Si mesmo — que tudo o que você precisa está Nele — você pode parar de se esforçar para alcançar algo e simplesmente começar a receber e a descansar na Pessoa gloriosa de Jesus Cristo. Você tem tudo porque você O tem.

Cristo É a Nossa Salvação Pessoal - Quando falamos de fé, é automático dizermos: "O Senhor Jesus é o nosso Salvador." E isso é absolutamente verdade! Ele nos resgata, nos liberta e nos redime. Mas vamos parar e considerar uma verdade mais profunda e ainda mais impressionante revelada pelo Rei Davi no Salmo 27:1, onde ele declara: "O SENHOR... é a minha salvação." (ARA).

Não é apenas que o Senhor age como nosso Salvador; Davi viu que o Senhor é o próprio estado de ser salvo. Jesus não é apenas Aquele que salva você; Ele é a própria Salvação viva e definitiva.

Essa revelação nos move de simplesmente confiar nas Suas ações para abraçar a Sua Pessoa. O Senhor Jesus possui ambos os títulos: Ele é o nosso maravilhoso Salvador e Ele é a realidade completa e gloriosa da nossa Salvação. Este é o coração profundo do presente de Deus para nós. Deus não distribui a "salvação" como uma mercadoria espiritual separada; Ele nos dá o próprio Senhor Jesus. Nele, o ato de salvar e o estado completo de ser salvo se tornam um só, tornando sua vida em Cristo completa, segura e eternamente abundante.

Cristo não é apenas o nosso Redentor, mas também a nossa Redenção. Ele não é apenas o nosso Santificador, mas também a nossa Santificação. Ele não é apenas o nosso Justificador, mas também a nossa Justiça. Ele não é apenas Aquele que nos torna sábios, mas Ele mesmo é a nossa Sabedoria.

Pai, eu me humilho diante de Ti e me rendo à magnífica verdade de que Cristo é o Teu tudo e, portanto, o meu tudo.

Eu entrego minha luta para adquirir "coisas" espirituais ou para me aperfeiçoar por meio de um esforço religioso. Eu confesso que procurei no passado por virtudes como coisas separadas, mas a Tua verdade libertadora me mostra que não existe "coisa" alguma separada de Cristo, pois Ele é a essência de tudo o que eu preciso.

Eu entrego meu velho entendimento e abraço a profunda realidade do Teu Filho. Eu O recebo agora como o Pão da Vida, o sustento para a minha alma; a Luz do Mundo, a verdade que dissipa toda a minha escuridão; o Caminho e o Modo, o caminho vivo que me conduz a Ti, a minha própria Vida, a minha Esperança e a completa Ressurreição da minha vida.

Eu descanso na verdade de que Cristo é tudo e em todos. Eu entrego minhas complexidades e preocupações, reconhecendo que, da Tua perspectiva eterna, Cristo é a única coisa. Eu paro de me esforçar e simplesmente escolho permanecer na Pessoa viva de Jesus Cristo.

Que a minha vida seja uma contínua e alegre rendição a Cristo, que é a minha Salvação, a minha Fonte e o destino glorioso de todos os Teus propósitos.

No nome poderoso de Jesus, o meu Tudo, eu oro. Amém.

3

Cristo é o Caminho, a Verdade e a Vida

Disse-lhe Jesus: Eu sou o caminho, e a verdade e a vida; ninguém vem ao Pai, senão por mim. (João 14:6)

Descobrindo Nosso Tudo em Cristo

Em um momento de profunda revelação que ecoa pela eternidade, Jesus nos declarou: "Eu sou o caminho, e a verdade, e a vida; ninguém vem ao Pai senão por mim" (João 14:6). Isso não é meramente uma declaração, mas um amoroso convite para o próprio coração de Deus para nós. Quando Jesus pronuncia estas palavras fundamentais, Ele revela uma linda verdade: o único modo de se conectar de verdade com o nosso Pai amoroso é por meio d'Ele, a própria essência da verdade divina é encontrada n'Ele, e a vida vibrante e eterna que nos é tão generosamente oferecida flui diretamente d'Ele. Ele é a nossa acolhedora entrada, o caminho claro para a presença de

Deus, a nossa verdade máxima e inabalável que nos guia em todas as estações, e a fonte inesgotável de onde toda vida verdadeira se origina. Cada fôlego que damos, cada passo da nossa fé e cada conexão que experimentamos com Deus é maravilhosamente possível por meio de Cristo.

Pois Deus, com amor sem limites e intencional, centralizou todas as coisas — todos os Seus propósitos, todas as Suas promessas e todos os Seus dons — em Seu amado Filho, Cristo Jesus. O que Deus nos concede tão graciosamente é o próprio Cristo. Nesta realidade gloriosa, verdadeiramente, nada mais tem o mesmo significado supremo ou poder transformador. No entanto, muitas vezes, na maravilhosa e contínua jornada da nossa fé, podemos inadvertidamente nos preocupar com as "pequenas coisas": talvez as tendências passageiras do dia, os "modismos" populares que se desvanecem com o tempo, ou até mesmo o costume de rituais que, embora talvez confortantes, não nos atraem para uma intimidade mais profunda com Deus. Essas coisas, embora não sejam inerentemente ruins, às vezes podem nos distrair da essência central e viva da nossa fé, potencialmente nos afastando da profunda proximidade com Deus pela qual nossos corações realmente anseiam.

"Eu sou o caminho, e a verdade, e a vida; ninguém vem ao Pai senão por mim" (João 14:6 - ARA). Isso não é meramente uma declaração, mas um amoroso convite para o próprio coração da realidade de Deus para nós.

É por isso que é um convite poderoso e libertador orar para que Deus nos ajude graciosamente a ver Seu Filho de forma verdadeira e profunda – a percebê-Lo não apenas com nossas mentes, mas com uma compreensão espiritual que transforma nossos corações. No seu nível mais puro, mais profundo e mais capacitador, a vida cristã é conhecer Jesus e continuar a conhecê-Lo mais profundamente. Não se trata principalmente de quantas técnicas espirituais dominamos, quão perfeitamente memorizamos doutrinas teológicas, ou mesmo de quantos milagres surpreendentes testemunhamos ou participamos. Embora esses elementos certamente possam fazer parte da nossa experiência, o coração vibrante e pulsante de tudo é um conhecimento pessoal, vivo e crescente do Filho de Deus. Quando realmente começamos a conhecer Jesus — Aquele que é o caminho, Aquele que é a verdade, Aquele que é a vida — nossa força, nossa paz e nossa capacidade de viver vitoriosamente fluem naturalmente desse relacionamento precioso e dinâmico. O presente supremo de Deus para nós não é uma coleção de coisas separadas, ou bênçãos temporárias que podem ser contadas; é Seu próprio Filho, dado sem reservas para o nosso completo crescimento. A conclusão gloriosa, a verdade central e mais libertadora de nossas vidas espirituais, é simples e bela: "conhecer Jesus". Este conhecimento não é apenas intelectual; é profundamente experimental e transforma a vida.

O Caminho de Deus: Um Relacionamento Vivo, Não uma Fórmula Estática

Esta profunda verdade — que Jesus é o caminho, o nosso belo e divinamente estabelecido "modus operandi" — sustenta e ilumina todo o nosso relacionamento com Deus. É crucial que nossos corações compreendam profundamente que isso não se trata de aderir a uma fórmula rígida, uma lista de regras do que fazer e não fazer, ou seguir um conjunto estrito de regras externas. Em vez disso, trata-se de abraçar uma Pessoa, uma conexão viva, vibrante e continuamente se desenvolvendo com o próprio Senhor Jesus Cristo. Esse relacionamento pessoal, maravilhosamente estabelecido e nutrido por meio da fé sincera em Jesus, não é um evento único e estático que acontece uma vez e depois é deixado de lado. Pelo contrário, ele cresce em uma jornada dinâmica e contínua de descobri-Lo e conhecê-Lo mais intimamente e profundamente a cada dia. Portanto, um crescimento consistente nesse conhecimento vivo de Cristo não é apenas benéfico, mas absolutamente essencial para cultivar um relacionamento mais profundo e profícuo com o nosso Pai celestial; é o caminho contínuo, empolgante e verdadeiramente transformador do discipulado.

Às vezes, em nossa seriedade e desejo por progresso espiritual, podemos ser tentados a buscar "atalhos" espirituais ou soluções rápidas, na esperança de poder ignorar o processo de um relacionamento profundo. Podemos ouvir histórias inspiradoras ou sermões poderosos e procurar pela fórmula secreta. Por exemplo, após uma mensagem poderosa sobre encontrar a vitória por meio de Cristo em vez de por meio do nosso próprio esforço extenuante, alguém sinceramente poderia dizer: "Eu me senti derrotado por anos, mas hoje, finalmente descobri um caminho para a vitória! Graças a Deus, agora eu sei como! É por meio do Senhor, não de mim mesmo!". Isso é verdade, mas se a verdade da vitória por meio de Cristo for aplicada em nossos próprios caminhos (nossa mentalidade e forças), então é apenas um método e experimentaremos a derrota novamente. A verdade de que temos vitória em Cristo deve ser experimentada por meio do caminho de Deus, que é o próprio Cristo — nós temos vitória em Cristo e por meio de Cristo.

Frequentemente, somos cativados e genuinamente inspirados pelas histórias de outros — suas experiências transformadoras de fé, suas vitórias e seus testemunhos da fidelidade de Deus. No entanto, às vezes, em nossa admiração, podemos inadvertidamente perder o elemento mais vital — a conexão espiritual genuína, profunda e muitas vezes não vista com Jesus que verdadeiramente alimentou a jornada deles e produziu seus frutos. Quando perdemos essa compreensão crucial, podemos nos sentir presos, desanimados ou sem ter o progresso espiritual que tanto desejamos. A verdade libertadora, o princípio central que precisamos captar com nossas mentes e nossos corações, é este: no fim das contas, não se trata do como — os passos, os processos, as técnicas externas ou as fórmulas — mas profundamente do quem — a própria Pessoa de Jesus Cristo. A questão fundamental se torna: com quem cultivamos uma conexão espiritual profunda, viva e dinâmica? Deve ser, sem reservas ou substituições, com o próprio Senhor Jesus. Em essência, estamos realmente andando no "caminho" que é Cristo?

Considere a distinção vital entre simplesmente crer a respeito de Jesus (uma concordância intelectual) e verdadeiramente crer em Jesus (uma confiança relacional), uma fé viva que nos transforma radicalmente. Uma pessoa pode realmente entender – ela se vê com humildade e honestidade, talvez reconhecendo áreas onde falhou, se sentiu perdida ou experimentou o quebrantamento. Nesse momento de consciência genuína e profunda humildade, ela entrega sua necessidade, seu quebrantamento e seus anseios mais profundos, confiando de todo o coração em Jesus para fazer o que parece totalmente impossível dentro dela. E nesse belo e corajoso ato de entrega, ela descobre uma paz incrível e inabalável com Deus, uma paz que transcende o entendimento. É uma experiência verdadeiramente transformadora, uma mudança profunda da luta ansiosa para o descanso alegre na Sua graça.

O princípio central que precisamos captar com nossas mentes e nossos corações, é este: no fim das contas, não se trata do como — os passos, os processos, as técnicas externas ou as fórmulas — mas profundamente do quem — a própria Pessoa de Jesus Cristo.

Então, outra pessoa sincera pode ouvir essa história poderosa, desejando genuinamente a mesma paz e liberdade. Ela pode orar fervorosamente para que Deus revele suas próprias falhas e tentar diligentemente crer e seguir o que ouviu. Mas, para sua confusão, nada parece acontecer ou mudar de forma duradoura. Por quê? Porque a primeira pessoa experimentou a fé real, uma conexão viva, ativa e intensamente pessoal com Jesus.

A segunda pessoa, embora inegavelmente sincera em seu desejo, pode ter inadvertidamente focado em replicar meticulosamente uma fórmula ou um método sobre o qual ouviu falar. Ela não se conectou de fato, no fundo do seu coração, com a Pessoa viva de Jesus. Ela pode ter entendido os passos intelectualmente, mas perdeu o coração vibrante e interno da questão. Um método, por mais bem-intencionado ou perfeitamente executado, sem a presença interior de Cristo, é como um vaso bem trabalhado, mas vazio; não é Jesus, e simplesmente não pode produzir uma mudança espiritual verdadeira e duradoura ou satisfação profunda.

É uma verdade libertadora entender que qualquer coisa espiritual que não esteja profundamente enraizada e fluindo de Cristo é, em essência, como uma coisa bonita, mas, no fim, sem vida. Devemos sublinhar profundamente este ponto vital. Às vezes, pessoas sinceras podem se perguntar em seus corações: "Como é estranho que outra pessoa creia em Deus e sua oração seja respondida, enquanto eu também creio e oro, mas muitas vezes me sinto não ouvido ou invisível? Por que Deus parece tão gracioso com eles e não comigo?" Pode parecer, às vezes, que Deus está mostrando parcialidade, mas a verdade mais profunda e compassiva é que aquilo em que podemos estar inconscientemente confiando pode ser meramente uma "coisa" – talvez uma técnica espiritual específica, uma abordagem particular da oração ou uma fórmula emprestada da experiência de outra pessoa – e, portanto, inerentemente carece de vida espiritual verdadeira.

Nem fórmulas nem métodos externos, por mais inteligentes ou atraentes que sejam, podem realmente funcionar no reino espiritual dinâmico; somente Cristo é vivo, vibrante e eternamente vivificador. Mesmo que alguém tenha aprendido meticulosamente um conjunto inteiro de técnicas espirituais ou doutrinas teológicas, não está, por isso, "educado" para ser um cristão, porque os amados filhos de Deus nascem do Espírito através da fé em Cristo, não são simplesmente ensinados ou treinados em um modo de vida religioso.

"Eu sou o caminho", afirma o Senhor Jesus com tanta força. Cristo é o nosso caminho, e Cristo é o verdadeiro e vivo método de Deus. Queridos amigos, perguntemo-nos honestamente:

Cristo é verdadeiramente o meu caminho, o próprio caminho que eu trilho diariamente, e Ele é verdadeiramente o meu método, a fonte e o meio de tudo o que faço? Ou estou, às vezes, me apoiando em um "caminho" ou um "método" que está separado da Sua presença viva? Podemos nos alegrar e dar profundas graças porque, se Cristo é genuinamente o método do nosso Deus, então tudo o que empreendemos será imbuído do Seu sucesso espiritual e produzirá frutos abundantes e duradouros. Mas se o que nos apoiamos é apenas um método – por mais bom, preciso e aparentemente incomparável que possa ser – se não estiver enraizado e fluindo do Cristo vivo, ele ainda permanece espiritualmente inerte e não tem valor espiritual duradouro. A razão para muitas orações que parecem não respondidas e testemunhos que parecem ineficazes é frequentemente encontrada no fato de não estarmos verdadeiramente tocando o próprio Senhor. Podemos ter copiado sinceramente os métodos ou práticas de outros, esperando por seus resultados, mas podemos ainda não ter nos conectado profundamente com o próprio Senhor.

Outro exemplo: Alguém que conhece genuinamente o Senhor estava compartilhando uma mensagem profunda sobre o livro de Romanos em um determinado encontro. Após ouvir a mensagem, uma pessoa compartilhou animadamente: "Hoje, finalmente entendi o caminho para a vitória! Agora tenho uma nova clareza. Creio que de agora em diante, não serei derrotado como antes." Essa pessoa havia recebido um método, um entendimento claro. Outra pessoa se aproximou do pregador e acenou com a cabeça levemente, uma contemplação silenciosa em seus olhos. Quando lhe perguntaram como se sentia, ele respondeu: "Não sei como descrever. Mas o Senhor abriu meus olhos. Embora eu não possa dizer que O vi com perfeita clareza, não ouso dizer que também não O vi." O que este segundo irmão obteve não foi meramente um método, um conjunto de instruções, mas um encontro interno e genuíno com o próprio Senhor. Consequentemente, ele manteve-se firmemente em seu terreno espiritual e experimentou uma transformação duradoura, enquanto a primeira pessoa, que havia recebido apenas um método e não o próprio Senhor, infelizmente pode enfrentar lutas novamente; pois o método sozinho, sem o Cristo vivo, não tinha valor duradouro.

Considere as palavras de Jesus em Lucas 18:9-14 — O fariseu, estando em pé, orava consigo desta maneira: Ó Deus, graças te dou porque não sou como os demais homens, roubadores, injustos e adúlteros; nem ainda como este publicano... O publicano, porém, estando em pé, de longe, nem ainda queria levantar os olhos ao céu, mas batia no peito, dizendo: Ó Deus, tem misericórdia de mim, pecador!

Cristo é verdadeiramente o meu caminho, o próprio caminho que eu trilho diariamente, e Ele é verdadeiramente o meu método, a fonte e o meio de tudo o que faço? Ou estou, às vezes, me apoiando em um "caminho" ou um "método" que está separado da Sua presença viva?

Muitas vezes, até mesmo a motivação sincera por trás de ouvir uma mensagem pode ser sutilmente errônea. Em vez de pedir humildemente ao Senhor por uma revelação divina para que possamos verdadeiramente vê-Lo, podemos tentar principalmente com nosso intelecto memorizar um método ou um ensinamento para levar conosco, esperando que isso nos traga sucesso espiritual. E mesmo que sigamos diligentemente esse método, podemos nos ver sem progredir em termos de vida espiritual verdadeira e interior. Às vezes, porém, parecemos ter um vislumbre, um momento de *insight*, talvez sem ter grande certeza para ousar dizer definitivamente que vimos o Senhor. No entanto, nesses momentos preciosos, nós O vemos, e tal *insight* interno e genuíno provoca uma mudança real e duradoura em nossos corações e vidas. Graças ao Senhor, este é o verdadeiro caminho – não que tenhamos meramente aprendido um método ou um conjunto de instruções, mas que chegamos a conhecer verdadeiramente o próprio Senhor. É claramente demonstrado a nós em Sua Palavra e através do testemunho do Espírito que o próprio Senhor é o método, o meio e o fim de nossa jornada espiritual.

Por esta razão profunda, então, devemos, ao ouvir uma mensagem, um testemunho ou até mesmo ao nos engajarmos com as Escrituras, examinar-nos honestamente sem julgamentos. A questão crucial é: encontramos verdadeiramente o próprio Senhor de maneira viva, ou apenas entendemos um método, um conceito ou um ensinamento? Não há libertação verdadeira e duradoura, nem liberdade genuína, em apenas conhecer um método, por mais preciso ou bem apresentado que seja. A verdadeira libertação, a paz profunda e a transformação duradoura são encontradas somente em conhecer o Senhor. Ouvir como Ele ajudou outros, embora muitas vezes inspirador, não nos salvará; é a nossa confiança pessoal e sincera somente no Senhor que é verdadeiramente eficaz e traz a salvação. As palavras que descrevem um método e as palavras que descrevem conhecer o Senhor podem às vezes parecer as mesmas na superfície, mas suas realidades interiores estão a mundos de distância. O Senhor é o Senhor da vida, a fonte e o sustentador de toda a existência, especialmente da vida espiritual. Quem verdadeiramente O toca, toca a vida – vida vibrante, eterna e abundante. Tocar o Senhor, somente Ele, em fé genuína e rendição, é o que verdadeiramente dá vida às nossas almas.

Cristo é a Verdade: Nossa Realidade Libertadora

O Senhor Jesus, em Sua magnífica revelação, não apenas Se apresenta como o caminho, o nosso caminho divino para Deus, mas também fala profundamente de Si mesmo como a verdade. Esta "verdade" é muito mais abrangente e dinâmica do que uma mera coleção de fatos, doutrinas ou declarações teológicas sobre Cristo. Não, a gloriosa realidade é que é o próprio Cristo quem é a verdade, a corporificação viva de tudo o que é real, autêntico e divino. Com que frequência, em nossa busca genuína por entendimento, nós, como cristãos, inadvertidamente tomamos o ensino e as interpretações de Cristo como as verdades supremas, quando, na verdade, a verdade não é simplesmente o relato de um conceito ou uma coisa, mas é a própria Pessoa de Cristo?

"E conhecereis a verdade, e a verdade vos libertará," diz o Senhor (João 8:32). Consideremos isso claro e honestamente: quantas verdades abstratas ou entendimentos intelectuais nos tornaram verdadeiramente, profundamente livres em nosso ser interior? A Palavra infalível de Deus afirma com absoluta certeza que a verdade nos libertará, mas quantas vezes a "verdade" permanece para nós apenas uma doutrina, um conceito que apreendemos com a mente, mas que não se traduz em uma experiência libertadora? Nossos olhos espirituais podem ainda não ter sido totalmente abertos para ver de fato Cristo como a Verdade viva.

Podemos ter falado sobre muitas doutrinas profundas por anos, talvez até uma década ou mais, mas ainda podemos não tê-Lo visto genuinamente nessa verdade. Podemos ter ouvido diligentemente ensinamentos profundos pelo mesmo período, e, ainda assim, podemos não ter tido esse encontro transformador. As pessoas podem ser capazes de falar com articulação sobre a doutrina da co-morte com Cristo, discutindo suas complexidades teológicas, sem realmente conhecer o poder profundo e libertador dessa morte em suas próprias vidas. Ou podem conversar com eloquência sobre a vida de ressurreição sem experimentar pessoalmente o Seu poder vibrante e dinâmico operando dentro delas. Se tudo com o que nos envolvemos e falamos é doutrina desvinculada do Cristo vivo, então, em essência, estamos lidando com algo que permanece intelectualmente estimulante, mas espiritualmente inerte, algo que, em um sentido espiritual, está morto.

Consideremos uma ilustração prática. Imagine que uma pessoa lhe escreveu uma mensagem buscando aconselhamento espiritual, nos seguintes termos: "Meu irmão pecou contra mim, e não tenho clareza se devo perdoá-lo. Portanto, peço que me instrua. Meu coração está bem tranquilo diante de Deus. Se você disser que devo perdoar, eu o perdoarei. Se você achar que não devo, então não o perdoarei." Sério, qual é a sua opinião genuína sobre a abordagem de um cristão assim? É uma resposta viva? Consideremos outro cenário hipotético: Suponha que a pessoa mais querida para mim se foi, e eu escrevo uma mensagem a outra pessoa perguntando o seguinte: "A pessoa mais querida para mim morreu; devo chorar a sua morte? Se você disser que devo chorar, eu chorarei; mas se você disser que não, então não chorarei." Certamente você, com sua compaixão humana natural, sorriria gentilmente ou até riria de tal pergunta, pois ela é profundamente absurda. Se uma pessoa chora ou não chora unicamente de acordo com o que lhe é dito para fazer, então nem seu luto nem sua falta de luto são reais. Ambos são falsos, desprovidos de emoção genuína, e são, portanto, meramente obras mortas, não um fluxo de vida autêntica. Em nosso relacionamento com um irmão, você perdoa a partir de um coração movido por Cristo, ou não perdoa. Sempre que agimos unicamente com base em uma doutrina morta, sem que a verdade viva de Cristo nos transforme por dentro, isso se torna um mero fingimento, uma performance que carece de vitalidade espiritual.

Queridos amigos, vamos compreender este princípio libertador: tudo o que não é Cristo vivendo em nós, ou não é o próprio Cristo como a nossa verdade — ou seja, tudo o que é feito unicamente com base em uma doutrina, uma regra ou um entendimento externo — é, no reino espiritual, obra morta. Não tem vida verdadeira fluindo através disso; não está autenticamente vivo. Você percebe a diferença crucial aqui? É uma diferença muito vasta, muito significativa, para passar despercebida em nossa caminhada espiritual. O "trabalho" externo frequentemente exige nossa memória, nosso esforço consciente para relembrar e aplicar um princípio; mas a vida espiritual genuína age espontaneamente, de uma fonte interior. Uma palavra falada a partir da verdadeira vida espiritual não é impulsionada pela nossa memória tentando recitar uma doutrina; ao contrário, é motivada por um poder divino e uma Pessoa viva dentro de nós. O próprio Senhor, não meramente a doutrina ou o ensino, deve estar em controle ativo sobre nós, guiando cada um de nossos pensamentos, palavras e ações.

É necessário que haja um dia em que Deus, em Sua graça, abra nossos olhos espirituais para percebermos de verdade que toda a realidade espiritual, todo o poder autêntico, toda a verdade libertadora, é encontrada somente em Cristo. Não somos chamados a tentar constantemente lembrar certas doutrinas e nos esforçar para agir de acordo; em vez disso, é Cristo quem vive em nós, e Ele é a nossa verdade. Portanto, quando Ele age através de nós, é vivo, espontâneo e genuinamente transformador.

Tudo o que é feito unicamente com base em uma doutrina, uma regra ou um entendimento externo é, no reino espiritual, obra morta.

Consideremos uma pessoa que foi profundamente ofendida por outra. Ela não conseguia suportar a ofensa e, por isso, repreendeu o ofensor com raiva em um momento de frustração. Depois, como muitas vezes acontece, sua consciência ficou incomodada; ela sentiu uma sincera convicção de que deveria procurar o ofensor e pedir desculpas. Mas ao relembrar os detalhes de como aquela pessoa a havia ofendido tão profundamente, sua raiva foi novamente despertada, e sua resolução vacilou. Enquanto isso, o fardo interior permanecia; ela ainda sentia que realmente devia um pedido de desculpas à outra pessoa, mas a raiva tornava o encontro cara a cara difícil. Então, ela decidiu escrever uma mensagem, acreditando que esta era a coisa certa a ser feita, a coisa cristã. Pegou o telefone e começou a escrever: "Sinto que foi errado eu ter repreendido você." Mas, mesmo enquanto escrevia, ao ser lembrada mais uma vez de como aquela pessoa que a havia ofendido tão profundamente estava errada, sua raiva voltou, fervilhando sob a superfície. Depois de esperar um pouco, tentando se recompor, pegou o telefone e continuou a escrever, completando o pedido de desculpas. No entanto, durante todo o tempo da escrita, ela ainda estava irritada, um ressentimento profundo ainda persistia em seu coração. Em todas as aparências externas, esta mensagem parecia ter sido lindamente escrita por um cristão, expressando arrependimento, embora nós que entendemos as realidades espirituais saibamos que foi o resultado de uma doutrina sendo aplicada, e não de uma vida espiritual verdadeira e espontânea fluindo. Embora ela tenha escrito um pedido de desculpas, seu coração permaneceu cheio de ira e amargura não resolvida. Se ela encontrasse essa pessoa, poderia oferecer uma saudação educada e apertar as mãos, mas, interiormente, a controvérsia não havia realmente desaparecido, e, portanto, suas palavras e seu comportamento não poderiam ser naturais, livres ou genuinamente calorosos. Percebemos agora claramente a diferença? O Senhor é a verdade. Se alguma vez for meramente doutrina ou um conceito intelectual, e não o próprio Senhor vivo, é espiritualmente morto. Que possamos perceber esta distinção profunda: em todos os assuntos espirituais, com o Senhor é vida, mas sem o Senhor é morte. Se uma coisa é feita como um belo resultado da Sua graça brilhando e operando ativamente em nós, então essa coisa está genuinamente vivendo, dando o fruto da Sua vida eterna.

Cristo é a Vida: Nossa Fonte Abundante

Dando sequência às palavras "Eu sou o caminho e a verdade", o Senhor prossegue com a igualmente vital declaração: "e a vida". Enquanto meditamos sobre isso, somos gentilmente lembrados de uma verdade espiritual fundamental: a vida verdadeira e divina flui de forma espontânea e sem esforço em obras impactantes, mas o nosso "trabalho" humano nunca, jamais, pode ser um substituto para a vida verdadeira. Devemos ser muito claros neste ponto fundamental: o nosso esforço ou as nossas ações não são vida — pois a vida é inerentemente sem esforço, um fluxo natural quando o próprio Cristo está verdadeiramente vivendo em nós. Quão frequentemente nós, como cristãos sinceros, podemos nos ver labutando e nos esforçando para incorporar virtudes espirituais! Como podemos ficar cansados e sobrecarregados por meio da nossa labuta diária para "ser" um cristão. Pode parecer que certas doutrinas são as mais rigorosas, pois parecem exigir que geremos de alguma forma a humildade, cultivemos paciência, nos forcemos a ser perdoadores e estendamos a longanimidade por meio da nossa própria força de vontade. Essas exigências podem literalmente nos esgotar, deixando-nos exaustos e inadequados. Muitos crentes sinceros podem concordar que ser um cristão é uma tarefa difícil, cheia de luta. Isso é especialmente verdade para os novos crentes, cheios de fervor, mas talvez sem o entendimento dessa verdade mais profunda. Quanto mais eles tentam em sua própria força, mais difícil e frustrante pode se tornar. E depois de terem tentado por um longo tempo, podem ainda não ter nenhuma semelhança verdadeira com o cristão vibrante e alegre que desejam ser. Querido leitor, se Cristo não é genuinamente a nossa vida, então, de fato, nos sentiremos compelidos a fazer todo o "trabalho" espiritual em nossa própria força; mas se Ele é vida, então não precisamos lutar dessa forma, pois a Sua vida flui naturalmente. Mais uma vez, afirmemos esta verdade libertadora: a vida é o próprio Cristo, e o nosso trabalho humano nunca pode ser um substituto para a Sua vida divina.

Existe um erro grave e muitas vezes generalizado entre os amados filhos de Deus. Muitos consideram erroneamente a "vida" como algo que eles devem fazer, alcançar ou realizar diligentemente em sua própria força, acreditando que sem o seu esforço, não haverá vida espiritual evidente. No entanto, o que todos nós devemos realmente perceber é que se houver a presença viva e vibrante de Cristo como vida dentro de nós, não haverá a menor necessidade do nosso próprio "fazer" extenuante, mas sim, que a vida divina fluirá natural e belamente. Considere por um momento a maravilha, sem esforço algum, de como os nossos olhos físicos veem e os nossos ouvidos ouvem. Nossos olhos veem da forma mais natural, e nossos ouvidos ouvem espontaneamente, não porque "tentamos" fazê-los assim, mas simplesmente porque há vida neles. Devemos ser muito claros neste ponto profundo: a vida espiritual verdadeira flui naturalmente em obras e virtudes, mas as nossas obras nunca, jamais, são um substituto para a Sua vida. De fato, às vezes o nosso "trabalho" em questões espirituais pode inadvertidamente provar a ausência da verdadeira vida espiritual ou revelar a sua fraqueza. A vida resultará genuinamente em bons costumes e conduta justa, mas bons costumes, por mais louváveis que sejam, não substituem a fonte da própria vida — Cristo.

Por exemplo, uma pessoa pode ser exteriormente muito gentil, moderada e reservada em seu comportamento. Alguém pode elogiá-la, dizendo: "A vida desta pessoa é boa, é louvável." Mas este elogio, embora bem-intencionado, pode usar a terminologia errada. Pois o Senhor diz: "Eu sou a vida". Por mais gentil, moderada e reservada que essa pessoa possa ser em sua disposição natural, se essas qualidades não fluírem genuinamente do próprio Cristo vivendo nela, elas não são verdadeiramente consideradas vida espiritual aos olhos de Deus. É perfeitamente correto dizer que essa pessoa tem um bom temperamento, ou raramente causa problemas, ou sempre trata as pessoas com gentileza e nunca briga; mas não se pode dizer dela, com base apenas nessas características naturais, que ela tem uma vida espiritual rica. Se essas coisas boas são meramente naturais, produtos de sua criação, personalidade ou autodisciplina, elas não são Cristo como vida, pois não vêm da fonte divina de Cristo.

Se Cristo não é genuinamente a nossa vida, então, de fato, nos sentiremos compelidos a fazer todo o "trabalho" espiritual em nossa própria força; mas se Ele é vida, então não precisamos lutar dessa forma, pois a Sua vida flui naturalmente.

Outras pessoas valorizam outro pensamento, uma conclusão diferente sobre a vida. Elas supõem que a vida espiritual é simplesmente poder. Ter o Senhor como nossa vida, elas acreditam, significa que Ele nos deu poder para fazer coisas boas. No entanto, a Palavra de Deus nos mostra de forma linda que o nosso poder espiritual não é meramente uma "coisa" ou uma habilidade que possuímos; é simplesmente o próprio Cristo. Nosso poder não é uma força abstrata para realizar tarefas; em vez disso, é uma Pessoa viva. A vida para nós não é apenas poder em um sentido geral, mas também profundamente uma Pessoa. É Cristo quem Se manifesta em nós, operando através de nós, em vez de usarmos Cristo como um meio para exibir as nossas próprias boas obras ou realizações.

Esperamos que possamos ver claramente que a vida espiritual verdadeira não é nem mera empolgação emocional nem meras palavras profundas e ponderadas. Palavras de sabedoria, ditos inteligentes, argumentos lógicos e dissertações ponderadas, embora valiosos, não são necessariamente vida em si mesmas. Portanto, não é surpresa que alguns perguntem: "Que estranho que a vida não é nem fervor nem pensamento elevado. Onde, então, podemos encontrar a vida? O que é a vida, afinal?" Confesso que não tenho uma maneira melhor e mais completa de expressar este assunto profundo sobre manifestar a vida do que dizer que é o próprio Cristo. Tudo o que podemos realmente dizer é que é algo infinitamente mais profundo do que a emoção passageira e muito mais profundo do que o pensamento intelectual. E quando alguém encontra genuinamente este "algo", é instantaneamente vivificado interiormente, um profundo saber interior e uma vitalidade despertarão. Este "algo" é chamado vida, e é uma Pessoa: Jesus Cristo.

Então, o que é verdadeiramente a vida? A Vida é mais profunda do que o pensamento; o nosso intelecto nunca pode captar ou superar plenamente a essência divina da vida. Ela também é mais profunda do que a emoção; nossos sentimentos, por mais fortes que sejam, são superficiais em comparação com a profundidade da vida verdadeira. Quer estejamos falando de pensamento ou emoção, eles são aspectos relativamente externos e temporários do nosso ser. O que, então, é a vida? O Senhor Jesus declarou definitivamente: "Eu sou a vida". Devemos ser cautelosos para não concluir apressadamente que realmente encontramos a vida quando tudo o que encontramos é uma espécie de "atmosfera", como uma atmosfera supostamente espiritual ou emocionalmente carregada em uma reunião. Somente Cristo é vida; o resto, em comparação a Ele, não é.

Portanto, precisamos aprender diligentemente a lição vital de conhecer verdadeiramente a vida em sua forma mais pura. Pois a vida não depende de quão entusiásticas são as nossas emoções, ou de quão múltiplos e extensos são os nossos pensamentos; ela repousa exclusivamente sobre se o Senhor manifestou genuinamente o Seu próprio ser dentro de nós. Não há, portanto, nada mais importante, nada mais central para a nossa jornada espiritual, do que conhecer verdadeiramente o Senhor. À medida que O conhecemos profundamente, estamos tocando intimamente a própria vida. Devemos ver diante de Deus o significado profundo e belo de Cristo ser a nossa vida. Aqueles que são facilmente excitáveis ou especialmente inteligentes não são necessariamente as pessoas que conhecem profundamente o Senhor. Conhecê-Lo exige uma visão espiritual, uma revelação interior pelo Espírito Santo. Tal visão é vida, e nos transforma milagrosamente por dentro. Se conhecemos verdadeiramente o Senhor como a nossa vida, percebemos a total futilidade, a bela inutilidade, de todos os nossos esforços naturais nas questões espirituais. Consequentemente, aprendemos a olhar amorosa e alegremente somente para Ele, confiando inteiramente em Sua vida interior.

Quando cremos pela primeira vez no Senhor, muitas vezes não percebemos totalmente o que realmente significava "olhar para Ele" na prática. Mas gradualmente, à medida que crescemos em graça e entendimento, aprendemos cada vez mais a olhar para Ele, reconhecendo com crescente convicção que tudo — cada virtude espiritual, cada vitória, cada momento de crescimento genuíno, cada aspecto da nossa realidade espiritual — depende inteiramente de Cristo, e não da nossa própria força ou esforço. No início da nossa caminhada cristã, era natural desejar possuir uma "coisa" espiritual após a outra; muitas vezes achávamos desafiador confiar Nele para tudo. No entanto, depois de aprendermos um pouco mais por meio da experiência e do ensino gentil do Espírito, recebemos um entendimento mais profundo sobre a necessidade de totalmente confiar Nele. Esta confiança não é primariamente no sentido de crer que Ele nos concederá item após item de uma lista de desejos espirituais, mas sim, no sentido muito mais libertador de confiar Nele para fazer o que somos absolutamente incapazes de fazer por nós mesmos. Quando nos tornamos cristãos pela primeira vez, éramos frequentemente inclinados a fazer tudo por nós mesmos, impulsionados por um medo sutil de que nada seria realmente feito, ou de que as coisas de alguma forma desmoronariam se não assumíssemos o controle e exercêssemos a nossa vontade. Assim, muitas vezes estávamos trabalhando, nos esforçando e labutando o tempo todo em nossa própria força. Mais tarde, ao termos os nossos olhos espirituais abertos para ver verdadeiramente o Senhor como a nossa vida, chegamos a um lugar de profundo saber interior de que toda a realidade espiritual autêntica é de Cristo e não de nós. Consequentemente, aprendemos a verdadeiramente descansar Nele e a olhar somente para Ele como a fonte e o sustentador de tudo.

O que é verdadeiramente a vida? A Vida é mais profunda do que o pensamento; o nosso intelecto nunca pode captar ou superar plenamente a essência divina da vida. Ela também é mais profunda do que a emoção; nossos sentimentos, por mais fortes que sejam, são superficiais em comparação com a profundidade da vida verdadeira.

Guardemos na linha de frente de nossos corações e mentes esta verdade gloriosa: em vez de nos dar um item após o outro, Deus, em Sua sabedoria infinita e amor sem limites, nos dá Seu Filho. Por causa desta magnífica realidade, podemos sempre elevar nossos corações e olhar para o Senhor com fé genuína e terno afeto, dizendo das profundezas do nosso ser: "Senhor, Tu és o meu caminho; Senhor, Tu és a minha verdade; Senhor, Tu és a minha vida. É com o Senhor com quem estou intimamente relacionado, não as coisas que o Senhor me dá." Que possamos pedir constantemente a Deus que nos dê a graça, a capacitação interior, para que possamos ver verdadeiramente Cristo em todas as coisas espirituais, em cada aspecto de nossa caminhada. Dia após dia, à medida que crescemos neste ver, nos tornamos cada vez mais convencidos, com uma paz estabelecida, de que fora de Cristo não há caminho verdadeiro, nem verdade, nem vida. Quão facilmente, em nossa fragilidade humana, podemos fazer de coisas — práticas externas, doutrinas, sentimentos — o nosso caminho, verdade e vida. Ou, podemos chamar uma "certa atmosfera" ou uma onda de emoção de vida; podemos rotular um pensamento claro e lógico como vida. Podemos considerar forte emoção ou conduta externa como vida. Na realidade, porém, estas não são vida em sua forma mais pura e divina. Devemos perceber, com um profundo senso de libertação, que somente o Senhor é vida. Cristo é a nossa vida, a nossa própria existência espiritual. E é o próprio Senhor quem vive essa vida em nós.

"Fui crucificado com Cristo. Assim, já não sou eu quem vive, mas Cristo vive em mim. A vida que agora vivo no corpo, vivo-a pela fé no filho de Deus, que me amou e se entregou por mim." (Gálatas 2:20 NVI).

Deus Pai, eu me humilho diante de Ti e confesso que tenho pecado ao buscar um caminho, um tipo de método ou uma fórmula à parte do Teu Filho, Jesus Cristo.

Eu me arrependo do meu esforço para adquirir "coisas" espirituais e outras virtudes através dos meus próprios esforços, deveres religiosos e práticas externas. Eu confesso que muitas vezes confiei em uma "solução" espiritual, olhando para a minha própria força ou para a vida de outras pessoas, em vez de olhar para a Pessoa viva de Cristo. Eu me arrependo de ter tratado a Tua graça apenas como um suprimento para cobrir minhas falhas, em vez de abraçar a Cristo como a Sua dádiva total e única, a provisão exclusiva para toda a minha vida.

Eu abandono a minha confiança em qualquer coisa separada de Jesus, pois creio na verdade libertadora de que Ele é o Caminho, a Verdade e a Vida. Eu O recebo agora como o meu Caminho, o caminho vivo que me leva até Ti; a minha Verdade, a realidade que me liberta; e a minha Vida, a fonte constante de tudo o que preciso. Obrigado por ter tornado a minha jornada da vida em um relacionamento íntimo com a Pessoa de Jesus e um lugar de descanso no próprio Cristo, o meu Tudo.

Em Seu nome poderoso, eu oro. Amém.

4

Vida de Ressurreição

Em um diálogo profundamente consolador e poderosamente revelador com Marta, Jesus declarou: "Eu sou a ressurreição e a vida; quem crê em mim, ainda que esteja morto, viverá" (João 11:25)

O capítulo 11 de João revela de forma maravilhosa como o Senhor Jesus deu vida a alguém que já estava morto — em outras palavras, como Ele ressuscitou Lázaro da sepultura. Ele certamente tinha a capacidade imensurável de ressuscitar os mortos e, de fato, fez com que um morto fosse ressuscitado. No entanto, em vez de enfatizar o Seu poder dizendo: "Eu posso ressuscitar os mortos", Ele declarou profundamente: "Eu sou a Ressurreição". Pouco depois dessa gloriosa declaração, Ele demonstrou poderosamente essa verdade, de fato, ressuscitando Lázaro.

Tanto Marta quanto Maria, as irmãs que estavam de luto, estavam presentes naquele dia monumental. Da perspectiva humana delas, imersas em tristeza e anseio, poderia ter parecido muito mais apropriado e consolador que o Senhor Jesus simplesmente dissesse: "Não se preocupem com a morte do seu irmão, pois Eu posso e vou ressuscitá-lo".

Nós também, muitas vezes, nos encontramos ansiando por palavras assim – uma promessa do que Deus fará por nós. O que frequentemente admiramos e antecipamos com entusiasmo é que Deus realizará atos extraordinários em nosso favor. Frequentemente, as nossas orações e expectativas diante de Deus estão focadas na promessa de que o Senhor fará isto e aquilo por nós, atendendo às nossas necessidades e situações específicas.

No entanto, o Senhor deseja especialmente que vejamos e compreendamos de forma profunda que não se trata principalmente do que Ele pode fazer, mas sim do que Ele próprio é, pois as Suas ações, por mais poderosas que sejam, estão sempre fundamentalmente enraizadas e fluem diretamente do Seu ser glorioso.

Considere o exemplo comovente de Marta. Ela possuía uma crença louvável no poder do Senhor. Ela disse-Lhe com sinceridade: "Senhor, se tu estivesses aqui, meu irmão não teria morrido" (João 11:21). E Maria também compartilhava uma crença semelhante no Seu poder (João 11:32). Mas, na sua compreensão humana, ambas as irmãs, embora sinceras, inicialmente falharam em perceber plenamente que o Senhor, Ele próprio, é a Ressurreição e a Vida.

Que possamos, com o coração aberto, agarrar esta verdade libertadora: tudo o que Deus pode fazer, cada milagre, cada provisão, cada ato de restauração, está intrinsecamente incluído em quem Ele é. As pessoas frequentemente não recebem o poder pleno e dinâmico de Deus porque ainda não conhecem completamente quem Ele é na Sua Pessoa gloriosa. Como a Escritura nos lembra de forma maravilhosa: "Ora, sem fé é impossível agradar-lhe; porque é necessário que aquele que se aproxima de Deus creia que ele existe, e que é galardoador dos que o buscam" (Hebreus 11:6).

> *O Senhor deseja especialmente que vejamos e compreendamos de forma profunda que não se trata principalmente do que Ele pode fazer, mas sim do que Ele próprio é.*

O que o Senhor Jesus deseja nos dizer aqui não é apenas que Ele é capaz de preservar a nossa vida, mas que Ele próprio é a vida; não apenas que Ele pode ressuscitar os mortos, mas que Ele próprio é a ressurreição. Peçamos a Deus, com corações humildes e sinceros, que abra os nossos olhos espirituais para vermos verdadeiramente quem o Senhor é. É absolutamente essencial que vejamos, perante a própria presença de Deus, que Cristo é verdadeiramente tudo para nós. Com uma compreensão tão profunda e transformadora, faremos um progresso real e duradouro em todas as áreas espirituais.

É absolutamente crucial que percebamos que em Deus não existe "coisa" alguma separada de Cristo, nenhuma bênção ou poder independente d'Ele! O nosso progresso genuíno nas questões espirituais depende profundamente da nossa verdadeira compreensão desta realidade espiritual: conhecemos a Deus em Si mesmo ou conhecemos apenas as coisas que Deus tem feito ou o que Ele pode fazer?

O tema central e mais profundo do capítulo 11 de João não é meramente um relato histórico de como o Senhor Jesus ressuscitou Lázaro, mas sim uma profunda revelação de como Ele próprio era a ressurreição para Lázaro. Será que vimos aqui a distinção fundamental? O Senhor é a ressurreição. Pelo fato de Ele ter sido a ressurreição para Lázaro, Lázaro foi, portanto, ressuscitado. Ele não tinha apenas dado a Lázaro algo chamado "ressurreição" como um presente externo; Ele próprio era a essência e o poder da ressurreição para Lázaro. Em outras palavras, o que o Senhor fez foi a manifestação externa, mas o que Ele próprio era foi a substância divina, a realidade viva por trás da ação. Não estamos sugerindo que o Senhor Jesus não ressuscitou Lázaro fisicamente; apenas afirmamos que Ele foi ressurreição para ele e que, portanto, Lázaro foi ressuscitado.

É de vital importância para nós entendermos que todas as obras magníficas de Deus em e através de Cristo estão profundamente incorporadas neste princípio singular e glorioso. Pelo fato de o Senhor ser essa "coisa" (essa virtude, esse poder, essa vida) em nós, portanto, nós temos essa coisa. É uma ordem divina: Primeiro, o ser (o próprio Cristo habitando em nós) e, depois, o ter (o fluxo espontâneo da Sua natureza através de nós). Muitos cristãos, com boas intenções, tendem a falar sobre Aquele que dá e as Suas dádivas como entidades separadas. Mas um dia, em um glorioso momento de revelação espiritual, descobrimos que Aquele que dá é a Sua própria dádiva, o dom máximo e mais precioso. Pois Deus não traz muitos e variados itens para nos dar em pedaços fragmentados; o que Ele generosa e completamente nos dá é o próprio Cristo. É realmente um dia abençoado quando os nossos olhos espirituais são abertos para reconhecer plenamente esta profunda verdade — que todas as coisas, todas as realidades espirituais, todas as virtudes divinas, estão profundamente fundamentadas em Cristo.

João 11 não é meramente um relato histórico de como o Senhor Jesus ressuscitou Lázaro, mas sim uma profunda revelação de como Ele próprio era a ressurreição para Lázaro.

Aqui, o Senhor declara poderosamente quem Ele é. Ele diz: "Eu sou a ressurreição e a vida" (João 11:25). Visto que Ele é a Ressurreição, não há problema algum para Lázaro ser ressuscitado, pois a fonte da ressurreição está intrinsecamente presente n'Ele. Acreditamos de todo o coração que o Senhor de fato ressuscitou Lázaro, mas a ênfase profunda estava em ter o próprio Senhor como essa Ressurreição. A ressurreição física de Lázaro é, na verdade, um fenômeno maravilhoso, um testemunho de que pode e será feita novamente; mas conhecer o Senhor Jesus como Ressurreição, como a própria essência de superar a morte, é uma questão de importância infinitamente maior e eterna. Muitas pessoas podem acreditar intelectualmente no Senhor Jesus como O que dá a vida, mas crer n'Ele verdadeiramente como a vida em si é outra questão, uma realidade mais profunda e transformadora. Ele não é apenas O que dá vida, Ele também é a vida em si. Ele é a própria vida que Ele dá. Ele é tanto o Senhor da ressurreição quanto a ressurreição em si. Assim que tocamos verdadeiramente esta verdade libertadora, compreendemos instantaneamente com um conhecimento interior que o que está em Cristo é vivo, vibrante e eternamente real. O que Deus dá universalmente à humanidade é o próprio Cristo. Esperamos e oramos sinceramente para que possamos ter pelo menos um glorioso raio de luz a brilhar em nossos corações, fazendo-nos perceber, no profundo do nosso ser, que o Senhor é verdadeiramente tudo. "Eu sou a ressurreição e a vida", declara o nosso Senhor. Estas duas magníficas realidades — Ressurreição e Vida — abrangem e incluem toda a Bíblia; portanto, conhecer a Ressurreição e a Vida em Cristo é realmente uma questão de grande importância espiritual e consequência eterna.

Cristo é a Vida: A Essência do Nosso Ser

No jardim do Éden, um lugar de tirar o fôlego, Deus, em Seu projeto perfeito, colocou o homem que Ele havia criado com tanto amor. Diante desse homem, havia duas possibilidades distintas, que representavam a escolha final: ele poderia experimentar a vida divina ou escolher a morte. Se comesse do fruto da árvore do conhecimento do bem e do mal, foi avisado de que certamente morreria; mas, se comesse do fruto da árvore da vida, possuiria e experimentaria a vida em seu sentido mais verdadeiro e pleno.

O homem que Deus criou era realmente bom, perfeitamente formado e inocente, mas ainda restava uma questão decisiva e crucial — a vida ou a morte, participar da própria vida divina de Deus ou permanecer em sua existência natural, embora boa.

Naquele momento, ele era perfeitamente capaz de pensar, raciocinar e se movimentar fisicamente, mas, fundamentalmente, ainda não tinha a vida no sentido espiritual que era representada pela árvore da vida. Não queremos dizer que ele não estava vivo naturalmente, pois, a julgar pela vida física e natural do homem, ele certamente estava vivendo bem. Gênesis 2:7 nos diz claramente que "E formou o Senhor Deus o homem do pó da terra, e soprou em suas narinas o fôlego da vida; e o homem foi feito alma vivente." No entanto, a julgar pelo que é profundamente representado e simbolizado na árvore da vida, ele ainda não havia recebido a vida divina como uma realidade espiritual dentro de si. Ele possuía o poder de pensar e sentir — funções que constituem as principais e mais vibrantes funções da alma humana — mas não possuía a vida, eternamente simbolizada pela árvore da vida. Aqui, por meio dessa narrativa fundamental para nós, somos instruídos de que a vida divina é infinitamente mais profunda do que a mera emoção e muito mais profunda e abrangente do que o pensamento humano.

Tudo o que é precioso e autêntico no Cristianismo parece ter a sua falsificação — uma sombra imitando a substância. Vemos falso arrependimento, confissões vazias, conversões superficiais, zelo passageiro, amor interesseiro, até mesmo obras enganosas como se fossem pelo Espírito Santo, imitações dos dons do Espírito Santo e, tragicamente, até mesmo vida falsificada. Quantos cristãos sinceros, em sua seriedade, podem inadvertidamente considerar um bom sentimento ou fortes emoções como a própria essência da vida! Eles podem erroneamente estimar que uma "certa atmosfera" em uma reunião ou uma voz alta e fervorosa está inerentemente cheia de vida espiritual. Eles lutam para distinguir entre a verdadeira vida divina e o mero sentimento, sem reconhecer que a primeira é infinitamente mais profunda, mais fundamental e mais duradoura do que o segundo. Outra classe de cristãos sinceros considerará um pensamento nobre e perspicaz, ou talvez até mesmo uma emoção forte e comovente, como vida. Se eles encontram em uma mensagem vários pensamentos instigantes, palavras intelectualmente interessantes e argumentos lógicos e louváveis, podem considerá-la a presença da verdadeira vida. Mas aqueles que são verdadeiramente experientes nos caminhos de Deus e que aprenderam de forma genuína por meio do Espírito nos dirão, com amorosa sabedoria, que a verdadeira vida é claramente mais profunda do que o sentimento passageiro ou o pensamento intelectual por si só. Além disso, a vida não é meramente ação ou atividade. Não é porque alguém é extremamente animado, externamente entusiasmado e perpetuamente ativo no ministério que ele pode ser necessariamente considerado alguém que está verdadeiramente "em vida". A pessoa pode, de fato, estar envolvida em muita ação, mas essa atividade externa, se desprovida da fonte interior, não pode ser rotulada como verdadeira vida divina. O homem, nesse caso, está trabalhando, se esforçando e atuando em vez de simplesmente viver o fluir espontâneo e sem esforço da vida de Cristo dentro dele.

A vida, portanto, não é nenhuma questão fora de Cristo; é o próprio Cristo. Se é meramente uma coisa, um conceito abstrato ou uma prática externa, está, em um sentido espiritual, morta.

Agora, não insinuamos, de forma alguma, que não há pensamento, nem sentimento, nem ação em uma vida vivida em Cristo; simplesmente afirmamos com convicção inabalável que a verdadeira vida divina não é meramente sentimento, nem meramente pensamento, nem meramente ação. Você pode ouvir de fontes distintas a mesma boa palavra bíblica, mas em uma pessoa você sente a presença vibrante da vida fluindo através de sua articulação, enquanto na outra, você percebe apenas um pensamento intelectual, por mais claro e preciso que seja. Você pode testemunhar uma resposta emotiva em uma pessoa, mas encontrar a vida verdadeira e profunda em outra. Muitos irmãos sinceros consideram certas sensações dentro deles como vida verdadeira, mas aqueles que aprenderam de forma genuína com o Espírito sabem que isso simplesmente não é verdade; os sentimentos são bons, mas passageiros e podem ser enganosos. Muitos também consideram certos pensamentos profundos dentro deles como vida, mas os crentes experientes, que provaram a profundidade de Cristo, declararão, com amor, que isso não é a verdadeira vida divina.

Há tantos que, em sua sinceridade, pensam que, por dizerem palavras semelhantes ou terem crenças semelhantes, eles também são os mesmos na realidade espiritual. Mas isso não é verdade. É totalmente possível que as mesmas palavras sejam mero pensamento em uma pessoa, mas verdadeiramente vida em outra, fluindo do próprio Cristo. "Eu sou a Vida", diz o Senhor (João 14:6). A vida, portanto, não é nenhuma questão fora de Cristo; é o próprio Cristo. Se é meramente uma coisa, um conceito abstrato ou uma prática externa, está, em um sentido espiritual, morta. A "vida" sobre a qual muitos cristãos falam e pela qual se esforçam é frequentemente apenas uma coisa que eles próprios produzem através de seus próprios esforços ou habilidades naturais, e não o fluir espontâneo da Sua presença divina.

Como nós realmente precisamos, desesperadamente, da terna misericórdia do Senhor neste aspecto crucial. Sabemos o que é pensamento, o que é sentimento e o que é atividade; no entanto, muitas vezes, nos falta uma apreciação clara e experimental do que a vida divina realmente é em sua essência. Que possamos, com corações humildes e desejosos, pedir ao Senhor que, graciosamente, nos mostre o que a vida realmente é — que nos conceda uma revelação de Cristo como a nossa vida. E em um dia glorioso, quando nos for dada uma revelação tão profunda pelo Seu Espírito, saberemos o que a vida é de forma natural e instintiva, não precisando mais de definições ou explicações e, então, nesse conhecimento, seremos verdadeiramente capazes de tocar o próprio Senhor como a nossa realidade viva.

E a unção que vós recebestes dele fica em vós, e não tendes necessidade de que alguém vos ensine; mas, como a mesma unção vos ensina todas as coisas, e é verdadeira, e não é mentira, assim como ela vos ensinou, assim nele permanecereis. (1 João 2:27)

Cristo é a Ressurreição: Triunfo Sobre a Morte

Voltemos nossos corações e mentes mais uma vez para a gloriosa verdade da ressurreição. Aquilo que encontrou o poder destruidor da morte e, no entanto, sobrevive milagrosamente, é chamado ressurreição. Tudo o que sobrevive à morte, tudo o que emerge vitorioso da sepultura, é ressurreição. A Morte, aquela intrusa indesejada, veio à humanidade depois que o primeiro homem, Adão, comeu o fruto proibido da árvore do conhecimento do bem e do mal. Desde aquele momento trágico, a humanidade tem sido totalmente incapaz de suportar a morte por sua própria força. Todos os que entraram no reino silencioso da sepultura jamais retornaram por seu próprio poder. Uma vez que se foram, eles nunca mais voltam para esta vida terrena. Na vasta extensão do universo, entre incontáveis pessoas que viveram e morreram, houve apenas uma, uma exceção singular e magnífica, que voluntariamente entrou na morte e saiu dela triunfalmente—e este, este Vencedor sobre a sepultura, é o nosso Senhor Jesus Cristo. Como Ele mesmo declarou em uma gloriosa revelação ao Apóstolo João: "Eu sou o primeiro e o último; e o que vivo e fui morto, mas eis aqui estou vivo para todo o sempre. Amém. E tenho as chaves da morte e do inferno." (Apocalipse 1:17-18).

O Senhor Jesus não está meramente *associado* à ressurreição; Ele é o próprio Senhor *da* ressurreição, a fonte e o poder por trás dela. A ressurreição fala de uma vida que passa pela sombria realidade da morte, mas não é, não pode ser, mantida cativa pelo poder da morte. A Bíblia usa a palavra "detida" ou "presa" para descrever vividamente o poder formidável da morte. As pessoas entram na morte e não conseguem sair novamente porque a morte, como um carcereiro implacável, prende firmemente todos os que entraram em seu domínio. Mas a morte, em todo o seu poder, não pôde e não pode deter a Cristo Jesus. Portanto, Sua saída da sepultura é chamada vida, um novo e invencível tipo de vida, e é também, e preeminentemente, chamada ressurreição. A ressurreição, em seu sentido mais profundo, é a vida divina que voluntariamente se submeteu à morte, foi posta na sepultura e, no entanto, está viva para todo o sempre, uma realidade perpétua e vibrante. Nosso Senhor Jesus é esta vida, esta vida de ressurreição, precisamente porque Ele esteve morto—tendo, em Sua obra redentora, entrado no inferno, no recesso mais profundo da terra, o reino dos mortos—contudo, Ele está vivo para todo o sempre, assentado à destra do Pai. A morte não teve poder para mantê-lo em suas garras; suas correntes foram quebradas, sua vitória desfeita. Ele sai da morte, deixando a sepultura vazia e seu poder vencido. E uma vida assim, uma vida que encarou a morte e emergiu eternamente triunfante, é chamada ressurreição. Assim, uma vida que carrega as marcas inegáveis de ter passado pela morte e, no entanto, está gloriosa e perpetuamente viva é a própria definição de ressurreição.

Algumas pessoas sinceras, ponderando os relatos bíblicos, perguntam por que está registrado no capítulo 20 de João que, após o Senhor Jesus ter ressuscitado dentre os mortos, Ele intencionalmente deixou o vívido vestígio dos cravos em Suas mãos e a marca da lança em Seu lado para Tomé tocar e examinar. Isto não foi um mero descuido ou algo que permaneceu; foi uma demonstração deliberada e poderosa do significado da ressurreição. O que o Senhor pretendia mostrar a Tomé, e através dele a todos os que creriam, não era simplesmente que Ele havia sido ferido e morrido, mas que havia sido ferido até a morte e, no entanto, eis que Ele está agora gloriosamente vivo, carregando em Seu corpo ressurreto o próprio vestígio do ataque da morte. No entanto, apesar dessas marcas, Ele é inegavelmente vivo eternamente. Isso, em sua realidade tangível, é chamado ressurreição—a vida triunfando sobre a morte, carregando as cicatrizes da batalha, mas vivendo em eterna vitória.

Essa realidade deve ser verdadeira, em um sentido espiritual e experiencial, em nossas próprias vidas como crentes que estão unidos a Cristo em Sua morte e ressurreição. Muitas vezes temos muitas coisas em nossas vidas naturais, nossas habilidades naturais, nossa autoconfiança, nossa força humana, que não carregam o vestígio de terem passado pela morte e, portanto, não podem, em um sentido espiritual, ser rotuladas como ressurreição. Somente aquilo que carrega o vestígio indelével de ter passado pela morte e, no entanto, está agora vivo, animado pela vida de ressurreição de Cristo, é chamado ressurreição.

A ressurreição fala de uma vida que passa pela sombria realidade da morte, mas não é, não pode ser, mantida cativa pelo poder da morte.

Não imagine que está tudo bem com você, em um sentido espiritual, se o que você possui é só eloquência natural, esperteza humana e capacidade inata. É bem possível que você tenha todas essas qualidades naturais—eloquência, esperteza e capacidade—sem o vestígio essencial de que a morte tenha operado nelas. Pessoas espiritualmente perspicazes podem julgar se há ou não vida de ressurreição genuína em operação, observando se o vestígio da morte, a marca da cruz, está sobre nossa eloquência natural, nossa esperteza humana e nossa capacidade inata. Um homem pode possuir grande talento natural e ser muito capaz em muitas áreas; ele pode parecer, em um sentido humano, muito vivo e vibrante. No entanto, pode não haver uma marca genuína da morte, nenhuma evidência de que a cruz tenha operado em seu talento, precisamente porque ele tem uma confiança tão profunda em si mesmo, dependendo de suas próprias habilidades. Ele confia que raramente, se é que alguma vez, erra, e muitas vezes tem certeza de sucesso em tudo o que empreende, apoiando-se em seu próprio entendimento e força. Esta pessoa pode possuir imensa autoconfiança, autossuficiência, auto segurança e auto força, mas tragicamente, ainda não tem a marca essencial da morte, o quebrantamento que vem do encontro experiencial com a cruz. Não queremos dizer que uma pessoa ressurreta, aquela em quem a vida de ressurreição de Cristo está em operação, não tem poder; o que estamos tentando afirmar aqui é que no poder de um ressuscitado, há sempre o sinal inegável de que a morte esteve em operação. Ele é capaz de trabalhar, ministrar, servir, mas não ousa, não vai, depender de si mesmo ou de sua própria força. Ele pode fazer muitas obras, empoderado por Cristo, contudo perdeu aquele toque de auto segurança que caracterizava seu homem natural, e sua própria força humana, através da cruz, foi transformada em uma fraqueza consciente que o faz depender inteiramente de Deus. Esta, esta profunda transformação, chamamos de ressurreição.

Em sua carta profundamente honesta e humilde à igreja em Corinto, o grande Apóstolo Paulo confessa o seguinte, revelando a marca da morte e ressurreição em sua própria vida: "E eu estive convosco em fraqueza, e em temor, e em grande tremor" (1 Coríntios 2:3). Estas não são as palavras de um homem fraco ou inseguro em um sentido humano, mas palavras ditas por alguém que realmente conhece a Deus, que encontrou experiencialmente a cruz e o poder da ressurreição. Quão trágico é que haja tantas pessoas aparentemente fortes e autoconfiantes entre os crentes que ainda não aprenderam esta lição vital de fraqueza e dependência de Cristo. Mas aqui está um homem, um gigante espiritual, que humildemente se reconhece estando experiencialmente em fraqueza, em temor e em tremor diante da magnitude da obra de Deus. Há, em seu próprio ser e ministério, o vestígio inegável de que a morte operou em sua força natural, abrindo caminho para o poder da ressurreição.

Consequentemente, na economia divina, a ressurreição e a cruz são eternamente inseparáveis. A cruz, em sua realidade espiritual, é um poder eliminador. Coisas que se originam de nós mesmos, nossas habilidades naturais, nossa autossuficiência, nossa natureza decaída, são totalmente incapazes de ressuscitar depois de terem passado pela cruz experiencialmente, pois estão perdidas na morte, seu poder quebrado. Somente o que passa pela morte e sobrevive milagrosamente, o que tem o sinal da morte sobre si e, no entanto, vive, animado pela vida divina, é ressurreição. A ressurreição, por sua própria natureza, pressupõe uma passagem pela morte, uma crucificação espiritual, e passar pela morte sempre elimina algo do velho eu, decaído.

Se realmente soubermos, experiencialmente, o que é a ressurreição, simultaneamente saberemos que a cruz é um poder eliminador profundo em nossas vidas. Quando passamos pela cruz, permitindo que sua obra tenha seu efeito, seremos livrados de muitas coisas que antes caracterizavam nosso homem natural. Nos tornaremos uma pessoa totalmente diferente, uma nova criação em Cristo, precisamente porque muitas coisas, muitos aspectos do nosso velho eu, terão sido despidos de nós, deixados na sepultura da cruz. Somente aquilo que tem a vida divina sobre si, aquilo que é nascido do Espírito, pode experimentar a ressurreição; sem a vida divina nisso, não há possibilidade de ressurreição. Por exemplo, no reino natural, podemos cortar um tronco de madeira em pedaços e enterrá-los na terra. Depois de muitos dias, esses pedaços estarão completamente apodrecidos e se tornarão totalmente inúteis, voltando ao pó. Mas se cortarmos um ramo vivo de uma árvore e o plantarmos na terra, se as condições forem adequadas, o encontraremos brotando e crescendo depois de um tempo, gerando nova vida. Um se apodrecerá e voltará ao pó, enquanto o outro brotará com nova vida. Tudo o que é espiritualmente morto, aquilo que é da natureza humana decaída, será eventualmente corrompido e passará; somente o que é espiritualmente vivo, o que é nascido de Deus e tem Sua vida divina dentro de si, será ressuscitado ao passar pela morte experiencialmente com Cristo. Minha vida com Cristo deve ser plantada, não enterrada.

Podemos nos fazer esta pergunta: Como sei que morri para mim mesmo? Como posso saber que a cruz realmente fez sua obra em mim? A resposta, embora simples, é profunda. Se o Senhor realmente trabalhou em sua vida através do poder da cruz, você perderá experiencialmente muitas coisas que antes o definiam em seu estado natural. Se você permaneceu essencialmente intacto desde que foi salvo, ainda sendo tão "rico" em suas habilidades naturais e tão "cheio" de autoconfiança como antes, isso indica claramente que a cruz ainda não operou plenamente em você, seu poder de subtração não teve seu efeito. À medida que a cruz opera em sua vida, você notará o grande trabalho de subtração ou limpeza que o Senhor realizou em você, um despojamento divino do velho. E, como consequência, o que você era naturalmente capaz de fazer antes, dependendo de sua própria força, agora você não é mais capaz de fazer da mesma maneira; daquilo que você antes tinha suprema confiança, você agora não tem tanta confiança em si mesmo, e naquilo que você originalmente tinha grande coragem natural, você ultimamente hesita, não em um sentido negativo, mas em um santo temor e dependência de Deus. Assim são as obras genuínas do Senhor provadas em uma vida. No caso de haver verdadeira ressurreição em sua vida, muitos itens de sua velha natureza, seu eu e suas expressões, devem ter sido deixados para trás na sepultura da cruz, já que as coisas lá, coisas de Adão, não podem possivelmente sobreviver à morte e emergir com nova vida.

Tudo o que é de Adão, tudo o que é nascido da carne, não pode viver ao entrar na morte; seu fim é a corrupção. Mas a vida divina do Senhor Jesus é bastante capaz de passar pela morte e sair triunfalmente novamente, nos trazendo com Ele. Este emergir glorioso carregando as marcas da morte superada, é ressurreição.

E eu, irmãos, quando fui ter convosco, anunciando-vos o testemunho de Deus, não fui com sublimidade de palavras ou de sabedoria. Porque nada me propus saber entre vós, senão a Jesus Cristo, e este crucificado. E eu estive convosco em fraqueza, e em temor, e em grande tremor. E a minha palavra, e a minha pregação, não consistiram em palavras persuasivas de sabedoria humana, mas em demonstração do Espírito e de poder; para que a vossa fé não se apoiasse em sabedoria dos homens, mas no poder de Deus.. (1 Coríntios 2:1-5)

Às vezes, coisas que foram perdidas na morte, coisas de verdadeiro valor que foram corrompidas pela queda, são recuperadas e restauradas em Cristo através da ressurreição. É como o ramo que, quando cortado de uma árvore, parece morto e sem vida, mas que, quando plantado na terra e nutrido, voltará a crescer e brotar, dando fruto. Assim, ao dizermos que temos o vestígio da morte sobre nós, a marca da cruz, não desejamos implicar que doravante não podemos mais falar nem trabalhar; é apenas que não seremos tão descuidados e autossuficientes tanto em nosso falar quanto em nosso agir. Quando uma pessoa é genuinamente tocada por Deus, sendo tratada pela obra profunda da cruz, ela se torna experiencialmente fraca e temerosa e trêmula, não de uma forma debilitante, mas com um santo temor e dependência, com o resultado de que não ousa dizer com confiança "Eu posso" ou "Eu farei" em sua própria força. Ela ainda fará seu trabalho, seu ministério, seu chamado, mas agora com o temor de Deus profundamente nela, dependendo do Seu poder. Ela continuará a trilhar sua jornada espiritual, só que agora ela anda *após Deus*, passo a passo, assim como Abraão andou passo a passo após Deus, sem saber precisamente para onde estava indo, mas confiando Naquele que o guiava. Em sua vida hoje, a marca da cruz é claramente perceptível, um divino transpassar e quebrar do velho eu. Ela foi transpassada por Deus; não está mais intacta em sua autossuficiência; ela carrega o vestígio indelével de que a morte operou nela, abrindo caminho para a vida de ressurreição. Esta, esta existência transformada carregando a marca da morte superada, é chamada ressurreição.

Se realmente soubermos, experiencialmente, o que é a ressurreição, simultaneamente saberemos que a cruz é um poder eliminador profundo em nossas vidas. Quando passamos pela cruz, permitindo que sua obra tenha seu efeito, seremos livrados de muitas coisas que antes caracterizavam nosso homem natural.

Hoje, Deus, em Sua sabedoria divina, se comunica com o homem no reino da ressurreição, e esta ressurreição, esta nova ordem de vida, inclui eternamente a cruz. Nada, portanto, que é do nosso homem natural, nosso eu decaído, pode estar verdadeiramente relacionado a Deus, pode ter valor espiritual genuíno, sem passar pela morte com Cristo. Tudo o que é natural deve ir para a morte; seu poder deve ser quebrado. Deus não pode e não vai contatar ou Se comunicar no terreno da ressurreição com qualquer um que ainda não morreu para si mesmo e ressuscitou em Cristo. Devemos morrer experiencialmente com Ele e então ser ressuscitados por Sua vida. A vida que recebemos, a vida que flui d'Ele, é vida de ressurreição, uma vida que passou pela morte e vive eternamente. Tudo o que aprendemos, tudo o que experimentamos, tudo o que fazemos que tenha qualquer relação genuína com Deus deve ser levantado dentre os mortos, deve carregar a marca da ressurreição.

Em questões espirituais, muitas vezes somos confrontados com um problema difícil e persistente: que as pessoas frequentemente servem a Deus sinceramente com coisas naturais, com suas habilidades inatas, seu zelo humano, sua própria força, em vez de servi-Lo com coisas de ressurreição, com aquilo que passou pela morte e é animado por Sua vida. Muitos têm zelo natural, um fervor humano, mas tragicamente, poucos têm zelo de ressurreição—um zelo que passou pela morte, foi quebrado na cruz e é ressuscitado pelo poder de Cristo, um zelo que não é do eu, mas de Deus. Muito zelo natural caracteriza o primeiro tipo, muitas vezes alto e demonstrativo, mas não o segundo, que é um fogo quieto e profundo vindo de dentro. Observamos vários irmãos trabalhando diligentemente e habilmente, usando seus talentos naturais, no entanto, sua diligência e habilidade são frequentemente do primeiro tipo—o natural—e não do segundo, o tipo de ressurreição, pois eles não passaram experiencialmente pela morte nessas áreas. Não podemos considerar isso como vida ou ministério de ressurreição genuíno se vivemos e servimos diante de Deus no poder de elementos naturais e ainda não crucificados.

Alguns perguntarão sinceramente: O que é o corpo de Cristo? O corpo de Cristo, a Igreja, é o reino, o organismo vivo, onde a ressurreição de Cristo é genuinamente atestada, onde Sua vida de ressurreição é manifestada e reina. Em outras palavras, tudo o que não é de ressurreição, tudo o que é do homem natural e não passou pela morte com Cristo, não tem parte, nem mesmo a menor parte, no corpo de Cristo; é alheio à sua natureza. A igreja não é o lugar onde você traz algo de sua esperteza humana e eu trago algo de meu tato natural, e juntos construímos algo. A igreja não é construída pela sua contribuição de um pouco de alguma coisa natural e minha contribuição de um pouco de alguma outra coisa natural, uma coleção de esforços humanos. A igreja, em sua essência divina, exclui todo o natural e aceita apenas o ressuscitado, apenas aquilo que é nascido de Deus e carrega a marca da cruz e da ressurreição. Sempre que o natural entra, sempre que elementos humanos entram, a igreja perde seu caráter divino, seu poder espiritual e seu testemunho. Não pode haver nenhum elemento não ressuscitado, nenhum aspecto não crucificado do homem natural, no verdadeiro funcionamento da igreja.

Muitos perguntam sinceramente como a igreja pode ser uma, como podemos experimentar a unidade genuína. Devemos perceber quão fútil é tentar alcançar a unidade espiritual verdadeira através de caminhos humanos, através de métodos organizacionais ou acordos externos. Os filhos de Deus precisam conhecer experiencialmente a cruz e lidar com a carne e o homem natural para chegar à unidade espiritual genuína, uma unidade que é produto de Sua vida, não de nossos esforços. Nenhum método humano é verdadeiramente eficaz a menos que as pessoas encontrem experiencialmente o Calvário, permitindo que a cruz faça sua obra em suas vidas, quebrando as barreiras do eu e do natural. Nenhum problema na igreja, nenhuma divisão, nenhum conflito, é verdadeiramente resolvido apenas por manobra e engenhosidade humanas; estas muitas vezes exacerbam os problemas. A igreja, em sua constituição divina, não permite que nem a carne nem o homem natural dominem ou tenham influência, pois ambos inevitavelmente danificarão sua saúde espiritual e seu testemunho. É bem verdade que a igreja requer as contribuições e ministérios de homens e mulheres, o exercício de seus dons e talentos; no entanto, deve haver o vestígio indelével da morte sobre eles, um quebrantamento da autossuficiência e uma dependência de Cristo. Utilidade no reino, acompanhada pela marca da morte, é chamada ministério de ressurreição. O próprio Senhor é a ressurreição, e Ele ardentemente deseja ter uma igreja de ressurreição, um corpo de crentes que vivem e servem no poder de Sua vida ressurreta, carregando as marcas de Sua cruz.

Se desejarmos sinceramente ter uma experiência de ressurreição tão profunda em nossas vidas e na igreja, então devemos buscar a Deus fervorosamente por Sua obra profunda e transformadora em nossas vidas. Talvez estejamos bastante familiarizados com muitos ensinamentos, muitas doutrinas, contudo, sem recebermos um golpe básico e fundamental do Senhor, um trato divino com nosso homem natural, tristemente permaneceremos essencialmente os mesmos, inalterados em nosso ser central. Às vezes escorregamos e caímos, cometemos erros e sentimos a dor, sim; contudo, isso dura apenas alguns dias ou alguns meses, e nos recuperamos, muitas vezes voltando aos nossos velhos hábitos. Mas se tivéssemos recebido o golpe básico de Deus, Seu trato divino, e sido suficientemente quebrados na cruz, não seríamos afligidos por meros alguns dias ou alguns meses; sustentaríamos aquela ferida espiritual, aquela marca da cruz, por toda a nossa vida. Seríamos para sempre, em um sentido espiritual, "aleijados" diante de Deus em nossa autossuficiência, e a marca indelével da cruz estaria sempre sobre nós, um lembrete constante de nossa morte para o eu e nossa dependência d'Ele.

Não podemos considerar como genuína vida ou ministério de ressurreição se vivemos e servimos diante de Deus no poder de elementos naturais e ainda não crucificados.

Muitos anos depois que o Apóstolo Paulo teve a visão ofuscante na estrada de Damasco, um golpe fundamental que o mudou para sempre, ele testemunhou com profunda humildade e convicção: "Por isso, ó rei Agripa, não fui desobediente à visão celestial." (Atos 26:19). Se o Senhor, em Sua terna misericórdia, nos alcançar e nos ferir severamente um dia, lidando com nosso velho eu na cruz, nosso velho eu nunca mais será capaz de se levantar em sua força anterior; a ferida, a marca daquele trato divino, permanecerá em nós para sempre, um testemunho de Sua graça. Visto que ainda é incrivelmente possível tocar, no Cristo ressuscitado, a ferida das marcas dos cravos em Suas mãos e da lança em Seu lado, tal ferimento, tais marcas de ter passado pela morte com Ele, nunca deveriam desaparecer na vida de todos os que hoje conhecem genuinamente o Senhor como ressurreição, como sua vida e triunfo sobre a morte. Experimentando esta ferida, este quebrantamento do eu, nunca mais ousaremos nos gloriar de nós mesmos e de nosso próprio poder; nossa confiança estará inteiramente em Cristo. Uma vez feridos pelo Senhor, uma vez tratados na cruz, não nos levantaremos mais em nossa própria força; nosso velho homem está crucificado com Ele. Que as marcas da cruz, a evidência de Sua obra transformadora, sejam cada vez mais evidentes em nossas vidas, um testemunho vivo do Seu poder de ressurreição.

Pretensão, performance espiritual, é totalmente inútil aqui; não tem lugar no reino da ressurreição. Pois o que é colocado por si mesmo, uma fachada de espiritualidade, logo será esquecido, desvanecendo-se como uma sombra. Mas uma vez que o sacrifício, nosso velho eu, é genuinamente colocado no altar da cruz e morto com Cristo, ele nunca mais se levanta em seu poder anterior; ele se foi para sempre na morte. Se alguma vez sofremos verdadeiramente este golpe básico, este trato divino na cruz, perceberemos com profunda clareza quão incapazes, quão acabados, quão totalmente "nada" somos em nós mesmos, separados de Cristo. Esta marca de morte em nós, este quebrantamento do eu, testifica nosso conhecimento e experiência genuínos da ressurreição. Conhecer a cruz experiencialmente é conhecer a ressurreição; são dois lados da mesma realidade divina. O que resta depois que a cruz fez sua obra, depois que nosso velho eu foi tratado, é vida de ressurreição, o próprio Cristo vivendo em nós. Oh! Quantas são as coisas de nossa velha natureza, nosso orgulho, nossa vontade própria, nossos desejos caídos, que nunca mais se levantarão, mas se foram para sempre depois de terem passado pela cruz com Cristo. Somente o que pode suportar a cruz, somente aquilo que é de Deus e tem Sua vida divina, possui verdadeiro valor espiritual e significado eterno. Tudo o que entra na sepultura da cruz e permanece lá é uma coisa morta, apta apenas para a corrupção; mas tudo o que sai do outro lado da sepultura, carregando a marca indelével da cruz, a evidência da morte superada, é ressurreição, vibrante com a vida de Cristo.

Busquemos à Ele fervorosamente, com anseio e corações sinceros, para que possamos realmente conhecer Cristo como nossa ressurreição, bem como nossa vida, não apenas como uma doutrina, mas como uma realidade viva e transformadora. Que o Senhor, em Sua graça, elimine muitas de nossas "coisas" em nós, muitos aspectos de nossa velha natureza e autossuficiência. Que Ele não apenas nos faça ter mais de Sua vida divina fluindo através de nós, mas também graciosamente nos conceda menos de nós mesmos, menos do nosso homem natural. Quão frequentemente nós, mesmo como crentes, vivemos de acordo com o natural, sem conhecer genuinamente a amorosa disciplina de Deus nem a obra profunda da cruz em nossas vidas. Precisamos pedir constantemente ao Senhor que seja misericordioso conosco, que nos conceda Sua graça, para que o natural, os aspectos não crucificados do nosso ser, possam ser gradualmente diminuídos em nós, enquanto o ressuscitado, a própria vida de Cristo, possa ser manifestado cada vez mais através de nós. Que a vida e a ressurreição sejam realidades gloriosas—não apenas teorias abstratas—para nós, moldando cada pensamento, palavra e ação nossa. Sempre que estendermos nossa mão para servir ou falar, que Ele graciosamente nos mostre se não há ressurreição nisso, alguma marca da cruz, visto que se tudo o que realizamos é apenas natural e carnal, é só um produto do nosso velho eu. Que Ele exponha nossa carne, nosso homem natural, pela luz penetrante da ressurreição, revelando o que não é d'Ele. Se ainda não conseguirmos ver, se permanecermos cegos para estas profundas verdades, que o Senhor seja misericordioso conosco e nos conceda a visão espiritual de que tanto precisamos.

Pai querido, eu venho a Ti com mãos humildes e abertas para receber o completo e magnífico presente de Teu Filho, Jesus Cristo, que é minha Ressurreição e minha Vida.

Eu reconheço e recebo a verdade de que minha vida espiritual não é sobre adquirir uma coleção de bênçãos avulsas ou esforçar-me para alcançar boas virtudes, mas é unicamente sobre viver e permanecer na Pessoa de Cristo.

Eu recebo a realidade libertadora de que minha velha vida está verdadeiramente morta, e minha nova e real vida de ressurreição está escondida em segurança com Cristo em Ti, meu Deus. Eu Te agradeço e recebo a certeza de que Cristo não é meramente O que me dá vida, mas que Ele é a própria essência da minha Vida, e porque Ele é a Ressurreição, eu recebo o poder para viver vitoriosamente agora mesmo.

Eu O recebo como a minha viva e definitiva Salvação, o Caminho que eu trilho, a Verdade que me liberta, e a fonte divina de Vida que flui através de mim espontaneamente a cada momento.

Eu recebo o fato inegável de que tudo o que eu preciso está corporificado Nele—minha Sabedoria, minha Justiça, minha Santificação e minha Redenção. Eu escolho parar de me esforçar para produzir coisas espirituais por mim mesmo, e escolho simplesmente receber a gloriosa Pessoa de Jesus Cristo, que é o meu Tudo. Amém.

5

O Pão e a Luz da Vida

E Jesus lhes disse: Eu sou o pão da vida; aquele que vem a mim não terá fome, e quem crê em mim nunca terá sede. (João 6:35).

Falou-lhes, pois, Jesus outra vez, dizendo: Eu sou a luz do mundo; quem me segue não andará em trevas, mas terá a luz da vida. (João 8:12).

Exploramos a verdade profunda de que todas as realidades espirituais estão enraizadas e são encontradas no próprio Cristo. Deus, em Sua infinita sabedoria e amor sem limites, nos deu graciosamente Seu Filho para incorporar e abranger cada uma dessas verdades divinas. Este não é apenas um conceito teológico; é um ponto fundamental e absolutamente crucial para realmente entendermos e navegarmos em nossa jornada espiritual.

Isso nos leva a fazer uma série de perguntas de profunda reflexão: Nossa experiência espiritual é apenas uma coleção de eventos isolados ou emoções passageiras, ou é fundamentalmente sobre Cristo vivendo e se movendo em nós? A justiça pela qual lutamos é simplesmente uma adesão externa a regras, ou é a própria justiça de Cristo imputada a nós e ativamente expressa através de nossas vidas? Nossa santificação é um projeto trabalhoso de autoaperfeiçoamento, ou é Cristo, que é santo, nos transformando continuamente de dentro para fora? E, por fim, nossa redenção é apenas um evento passado de ter sido salvo do pecado, ou é Cristo, nosso Redentor, ativo e continuamente nos libertando e nos tornando completos em cada aspecto do nosso ser?

Muitas vezes, falamos sobre "o caminho", mas esse caminho pode não ser o próprio Cristo. Da mesma forma, podemos discutir conceitos profundos como verdade e vida sem necessariamente nos referirmos a Cristo como sua fonte e corporificação suprema. Em resumo, frequentemente nos encontramos acumulando muitas "coisas" espirituais que estão, em essência, separadas de Cristo. Isso cria um desafio espiritual significativo para os filhos de Deus, pois pode levar a uma experiência de fé fragmentada e menos poderosa. Podemos confessar prontamente com a boca que Cristo é o centro absoluto de tudo—o Alfa e o Ômega—contudo, em nossa vida diária, inadvertidamente dependemos de uma infinidade de outras coisas, acreditando, talvez sutilmente, que estas podem de alguma forma nos ajudar a viver verdadeiramente o nosso chamado como cristãos.

> Cristo não é meramente a fonte das bênçãos;
> Ele é a própria essência delas. Pois Ele é a
> totalidade, a soma e a completa corporificação
> de todas as realidades espirituais.

Precisamos desesperadamente que nossas mentes sejam renovadas pelo Espírito Santo para que possamos entender que, à parte de Cristo, Deus não tem a intenção de que tenhamos uma coleção das chamadas "coisas" espirituais que operam de forma independente. De acordo com o plano divino e perfeito de Deus, existem de fato "coisas" que são essenciais para a nossa caminhada espiritual, mas estas "coisas" são o próprio Cristo. Ele não é meramente a fonte das bênçãos; Ele é a própria essência delas. Pois Cristo é a totalidade, a soma e a completa corporificação de todas as realidades espirituais.

Considere isto: Cristo é a nossa justiça—Ele não nos deu apenas uma justiça externa e avulsa para vestirmos. Cristo é a nossa santificação—Ele não nos concedeu meramente um poder ou um método para nos tornar santos; Ele é a nossa santidade, continuamente trabalhando em nós. Cristo é a nossa redenção— Ele não nos ofereceu simplesmente uma redenção como uma transação; Ele é o nosso Redentor, o próprio ato e a realidade contínua de nossa liberdade. Cristo é o caminho—Ele não abriu apenas outro caminho para andarmos; Ele é o próprio caminho vivo e dinâmico. Cristo é a verdade—Ele não apresentou apenas alguma verdade para entendermos intelectualmente; Ele é a verdade viva e libertadora que nos transforma. E, profundamente, Cristo é a vida—Ele não nos concedeu apenas uma coisa chamada vida; Ele é a nossa própria existência espiritual, vibrante e eterna. Esta compreensão muda nosso foco de lutar por atributos espirituais desconectados para abraçar a Pessoa de Cristo como nosso provedor todo-suficiente.

À medida que caminhamos no caminho de Deus, descobriremos cada vez mais que, entre toda a graça de Deus, há apenas uma graça, e entre todos os dons de Deus, há apenas um dom. Essa graça é Cristo, e esse dom também é Cristo. Graças a Deus, dia após dia Ele está nos revelando quão verdadeiramente abrangente é Cristo. Anteriormente, pensávamos no Senhor como nosso Salvador; agora podemos declarar que Ele não é apenas nosso Salvador, mas também nossa própria salvação. Isso parece estranho para você? Não, esta é uma profunda realidade. Pois estamos continuamente descobrindo que Cristo é a própria essência da provisão de Deus.

Se separarmos erroneamente o que o Senhor Jesus dá do que Ele é—separar a dádiva daquele que a dá—sofreremos muito em nossas vidas espirituais. Um erro como este nos impedirá de nos conectarmos verdadeiramente com a fonte da vida. Com isso em mente, desejamos ver mais de Cristo como nossas "coisas" abrangendo tudo. Em João 6:35 e 8:12, o Senhor nos diz que Ele é o Pão da Vida e também a Luz da Vida. Vamos explorar cada um destes por sua vez.

É uma bela jornada de fé realmente compreender esta verdade fundamental: cada bênção espiritual, cada atributo divino, cada aspecto de nossa caminhada com Deus não é uma "coisa" separada dada *por* Cristo, mas é profundamente o *próprio Cristo* habitando em nós. Quando falamos sobre nossa experiência com Deus, não é apenas uma série de eventos ou sentimentos; é Cristo vivendo e se movendo em nós. Nossa justiça não é meramente um *status* que alcançamos; é a justiça perfeita de Cristo imputada a nós e expressa através de nós. Nossa santificação não é apenas um processo de se tornar santo; é Cristo, que é santo, nos tornando semelhantes a Ele. Nossa redenção não é apenas um evento passado de ser salvo; é Cristo, nosso Redentor, continuamente nos libertando e nos tornando completos.

O desafio que frequentemente enfrentamos como filhos de Deus é que tendemos a compartimentalizar nossa fé, buscando "coisas espirituais" avulsas fora da Pessoa todo-suficiente de Cristo. Podemos correr atrás de métodos, doutrinas ou experiências, esperando que preencham um vazio, quando, na verdade, o próprio Cristo é a resposta completa. Nossas mentes precisam desesperadamente ser renovadas pelo Espírito Santo para compreender plenamente que a intenção divina de Deus é que Cristo seja tudo para nós. Existem de fato "coisas" no plano de Deus, mas estas "coisas" não estão separadas de Cristo; elas são Cristo em Sua plenitude. Ele é a soma total de todas as realidades espirituais, a corporificação máxima de toda graça e dom.

Esta revelação profunda transforma nossa perspectiva. Nós não apenas recebemos a graça *de* Cristo; Cristo *é* a nossa graça. Nós não apenas recebemos dons *d'Ele*; Cristo *é* o dom supremo. Dia após dia, à medida que caminhamos com Ele, o Espírito Santo revela amorosamente quão verdadeiramente abrangente é Cristo. Antes, O víamos como nosso Salvador, e de fato Ele é! Mas agora, podemos declarar com alegria ainda maior que Ele não é apenas nosso Salvador, mas também nossa própria salvação—o processo e a realidade completos de sermos salvos. Isso não é estranho; é um fato glorioso e libertador! Estamos continuamente descobrindo que Cristo *é* a própria essência da provisão ilimitada de Deus para nós, suprindo cada uma de nossas necessidades e excedendo todas as nossas expectativas. Quando realmente abraçamos isso, nossas vidas espirituais florescem e nos conectamos com a fonte inesgotável da própria vida.

Cristo é o Pão da Vida

"E Jesus lhes disse: Eu sou o pão da vida; aquele que vem a mim não terá fome, e quem crê em mim nunca terá sede." (Jo 6:35).

O Senhor declara: "Eu sou o pão da vida." Ele disse estas palavras poderosas às pessoas em Cafarnaum que estavam atrás dele, esperando que Ele as alimentasse com pão físico. Mas Jesus, em Sua sabedoria, revelou uma verdade mais profunda: "Eu sou o pão da vida." Ele não é apenas Aquele que dá o pão da vida; Ele é esse pão. Que realidade gloriosa: a dádiva e O que a dá são um, perfeitamente unidos! Graças a Deus, Cristo é tanto a dádiva suprema de Deus quanto o Senhor que graciosamente a dá.

O que o "pão" significa na Bíblia? Ele representa de forma maravilhosa a satisfação, pois a Escritura frequentemente usa a metáfora da fome para ilustrar a profunda insatisfação humana que pode afligir nossas almas. Para que nossos anseios humanos mais profundos—nossa fome espiritual—sejam verdadeiramente satisfeitos, precisamos deste "pão" divino. Esta não é apenas uma metáfora; aponta para uma necessidade fundamental dentro de nós.

Se os filhos de Deus possuem a força para perseverar através dos desafios da vida e, em última análise, terminar sua jornada espiritual, isso depende significativamente de sua satisfação interior. Se nos sentimos verdadeiramente satisfeitos e nutridos em nosso espírito hoje, teremos a força e a resiliência necessárias para o dia que está por vir. Por outro lado, se sentimos um vazio interior, um profundo vácuo muito parecido com um balão que murchou, podemos ter que lutar imensamente para seguir em frente, sentindo-nos esgotados e sem propósito. Não é que a vida espiritual esteja totalmente ausente em tais momentos, mas sim que este inexplicável e profundo sentimento de satisfação é o que realmente nos capacita a avançar, a suportar e a completar o curso divino estabelecido diante de nós.

Cristo não é apenas Aquele que dá o pão da vida;
Ele é esse pão. Que realidade gloriosa: a dádiva
e O que a dá são um, perfeitamente unidos!

Então, o que é este "pão" para os filhos de Deus? O próprio Senhor Jesus declara: "Eu sou o pão da vida." Esta declaração profunda revela que o Senhor Jesus não apenas sustenta nossa vida espiritual, mas também é essa mesma vida, a fonte e a essência dela. Muitos cristãos frequentemente limitam sua compreensão de nutrição espiritual a práticas como uma hora de oração ou uma hora de leitura da Bíblia. Embora estas sejam de fato disciplinas espirituais maravilhosas e vitais, às vezes elas perdem a verdade profunda e abrangente de que seu "alimento" verdadeiro e essencial é o próprio Senhor Jesus. Não estamos sugerindo que a oração ou a leitura da Bíblia sejam sem importância; em vez disso, enfatizamos a declaração direta do Senhor Jesus: Ele *é* "o pão da vida"—o que significa que o alimento divino que dá vida, a própria essência do sustento espiritual, não é outro senão o próprio Senhor! Ele é a provisão viva e dinâmica para toda necessidade espiritual.

Muitas vezes, os filhos de Deus se sentem insatisfeitos porque não compreenderam totalmente Cristo como o pão da vida. Frequentemente encontramos indivíduos que estão espiritualmente famintos e descontentes. Parecem infelizes com tudo, da manhã à noite, consumidos pela insatisfação. Certamente não queremos encorajar a arrogância ou o autossatisfação. No entanto, acreditamos que existe uma clara distinção entre o orgulho da autossatisfação e ser genuinamente alimentado e contente em Cristo. Alguns indivíduos, tendo sido profundamente tocados por Deus, vivem diante d'Ele em humildade e reverência. Não têm o menor vestígio de orgulho, mas verdadeiramente se conectaram com o Senhor e, ao fazê-lo, estão completamente nutridos. Eles possuem uma profunda satisfação na presença de Deus, e essa satisfação se torna a sua força.

Como, então, podemos ser totalmente alimentados e satisfeitos? Devemos entender que toda verdadeira satisfação está intimamente conectada a Cristo. Toda nutrição genuína é encontrada na própria vida. Cristo é o pão da vida! Sempre que nos conectamos verdadeiramente com esta vida divina, experimentamos imediatamente uma profunda satisfação. Inversamente, quando agimos contra esta vida, sentimos instantaneamente um "esvaziamento" ou vazio espiritual, uma profunda sensação de esgotamento que impede nosso progresso espiritual. Vamos ilustrar esta profunda verdade de obter satisfação com alguns exemplos práticos da Escritura e da experiência cotidiana.

Imagine alguém dizendo: "Estou trabalhando há mais de um ano, totalmente ocupado, correndo de lá para cá, constantemente engajado em várias atividades. Estive tão sobrecarregado que agora me sinto completamente vazio por dentro, totalmente esgotado de vitalidade espiritual. Estou espiritualmente faminto e anseio por um lugar de avivamento, uma fonte de força e propósito renovados." Este sentimento é comum entre aqueles que se esforçam em sua própria força. No entanto, em João, no Capítulo 4, encontramos um lindo contraste com este sentimento na vida de Jesus. O Senhor Jesus, cansado de Sua jornada, sentou-se junto ao poço de Jacó. Seus discípulos tinham ido à cidade para comprar comida, sugerindo que o Senhor estava de fato com fome física. Ali, Ele encontrou uma mulher samaritana. Era a vontade divina de Deus que Ele falasse com ela e lhe trouxesse salvação, uma tarefa que Ele abraçou fielmente. Ele fez exatamente o que Deus queria que Ele fizesse. Quando Seus discípulos voltaram com a comida, eles o chamaram para comer. Mas Ele lhes disse: "Tenho uma comida para comer que vós não conheceis." Eles, naturalmente, pensaram que outra pessoa Lhe havia trazido comida, falhando em compreender a realidade espiritual mais profunda. Consequentemente, Ele lhes revelou claramente: "A minha comida é fazer a vontade daquele que me enviou, e realizar a sua obra" (João 4:34). Esta poderosa declaração destaca que o verdadeiro alimento espiritual não vem do sustento físico ou do esforço humano, mas do alinhamento e cumprimento da vontade divina de Deus.

Deste poderoso incidente na vida de nosso Senhor, podemos com alegria concluir que o verdadeiro trabalho espiritual deve nos *encher*, e não nos deixar vazios e famintos! No trabalho espiritual genuíno, toda vez que servimos, devemos sentir uma sensação de plenitude. Se a fome segue consistentemente o nosso trabalho, algo pode estar errado. Se, após trabalhar para o Senhor, nos sentimos fracos, isso indica um problema com esse esforço específico. Pois, se andamos de acordo com a vontade de Deus e não em nossa própria força, devemos nos sentir fortalecidos, e não esgotados. Quantas vezes empreendemos tarefas, não porque estamos verdadeiramente preparados diante do Senhor, mas porque a necessidade externa parece esmagadora ou a persuasão de fora é forte. Em tais empreendimentos, experimentamos um desmoronamento interior que nos deixa esgotados após o trabalho. Este é um sinal claro de que algo não está certo entre nós e o Senhor. Todos os trabalhos realizados fora da vontade de Deus, em última análise, levam a uma maior fome espiritual. Portanto, devemos fazer diligentemente a vontade de Deus para experimentar a verdadeira satisfação.

É uma percepção maravilhosa que nem um poderoso retiro espiritual nem um profundo ensinamento bíblico, em si mesmos, são nossa fonte suprema de sustento; só Cristo é o nosso alimento verdadeiro e completo! Se Cristo é de fato o nosso alimento espiritual, então devemos reavaliar a ideia de que trabalhar até a exaustão, apenas para então buscar reabastecimento em um retiro, é o normal para suprir nossas necessidades espirituais. Da mesma forma, não devemos nos sentir esgotados depois de compartilhar a nossa fé, apenas para então buscar desesperadamente novos ensinamentos para reabastecer nossas reservas espirituais.

> *O verdadeiro alimento espiritual não vem do sustento físico ou do esforço humano, mas do alinhamento e cumprimento da vontade divina de Deus.*

Em vez disso, quer estejamos ativamente engajados no ministério ou simplesmente navegando em nossa vida diária, toda vez que nos levantamos para falar por Cristo, devemos estar tão transbordantes de Suas palavras e força interior que não apenas aqueles que nos ouvem são profundamente alimentados, mas nós mesmos também somos profundamente sustentados! Isso acontece porque é o próprio Senhor que trabalha poderosamente em nós. Quando nos conectamos verdadeiramente com Ele, não nos sentiremos vazios ao completar nossas tarefas, mas sim uma plenitude profunda e duradoura se instalará em nossos corações.

É maravilhoso perceber que muitas vezes estamos enganados se consideramos o mero descanso, ou simplesmente ouvir um sermão, ou participar de um retiro espiritual como o *único* meio de sermos preenchidos. Obter alimento verdadeiro, que dá vida, e nutrição espiritual é humildemente permitir que o Senhor realize em nós o que Ele deseja realizar. O Senhor que habita graciosamente em nós nos capacita a tocar em Sua própria vida, e esta conexão íntima por si só nos faz sentir profunda e eternamente cheios por dentro, prontos para enfrentar qualquer desafio com Sua força e alegria.

Na experiência espiritual, não são os que estão de folga que verdadeiramente "comem"; pelo contrário, comemos *mais* quando estamos ativamente engajados! Somos nutridos enquanto estamos ocupados. Se estamos andando na vontade de Deus, quanto mais ocupados, mais espiritualmente "comemos." E, consequentemente, não ficaremos exaustos ou nos sentiremos vazios por causa de muito esforço.

"Mas os que esperam no Senhor renovarão as forças, subirão com asas como águias; correrão, e não se cansarão; caminharão, e não se fatigarão." (Isaías 40:31).

Muitos de vocês podem, sem dúvida, testemunhar isso. Imagine, por exemplo, um dia em que você sai com entusiasmo para compartilhar com outra pessoa, falando com grande paixão e convicção. No entanto, apesar de seus esforços sinceros, você não sente nenhum movimento ou unção divina fluindo através de você. Após apenas cinco ou dez minutos, para sua surpresa, você começa a sentir uma sensação perturbadora de que algo está errado. Logo você se pega desejando mudar a direção de sua conversa, percebendo com um crescente desconforto que simplesmente não pode continuar como antes. O resultado desanimador é que você se sente totalmente vazio e esgotado quando finalmente se vai. Exteriormente, pode não ter havido nada de errado com suas palavras ou sua atitude; você realmente tentou o seu melhor para ajudar aquela pessoa. No entanto, estranhamente, você ficou mais vazio e mais esgotado à medida que continuava a falar. Quando você finalmente teve que ir embora, uma pesada sensação de fardo se instalou sobre você, quase como se tivesse cometido um pecado. Às vezes, você pode até ter observado um pequeno sucesso exterior, ou talvez tido a sensação passageira de que tinha se saído muito bem; no entanto, quando esses sentimentos externos inevitavelmente passam, você é deixado com uma profunda sensação de vazio e fome espiritual interior. Quão verdadeiro é que sempre que você avança em sua própria força, confiando apenas em suas próprias habilidades, apesar de algum grau de sucesso exterior, você acabará se sentindo como um balão furado, desinflado e sem vitalidade espiritual.

Você já se sentiu como se tivesse ficado completamente sem ar espiritual, faltando o próprio sopro da vida de Deus dentro de você? Se você anda de acordo com seus próprios pensamentos, confiando em sua própria sabedoria e entendimento, em vez de seguir o Senhor com humildade e reverência com um profundo senso de dependência, por melhores e bem-intencionados que sejam seus esforços, você sempre acabará se sentindo esgotado—faltando o verdadeiro impacto e poder espiritual. Quanto mais você trabalha em sua própria força, menos significativo e satisfatório isso se torna para você. Quanto mais você continua neste caminho, mais vazio e cansado você se sente. Em uma situação tão desafiadora, você frequentemente se sentirá ainda pior se receber elogios de outras pessoas, pois isso destaca a desconexão interna que você experimenta. Você pode até se encontrar desgostando de seus próprios esforços. Isso demonstra claramente que tal trabalho, embora talvez bem-intencionado, não é verdadeiro alimento espiritual, pois falha em satisfazer genuinamente os anseios mais profundos de sua alma. Mas anime-se, pois há um caminho melhor—um caminho de permanecer em Cristo, nossa fonte verdadeira e inesgotável de vida e satisfação.

Consideremos outro exemplo, embora mais profundo, que ilumina este princípio. Muitas vezes, nos encontramos fazendo o que genuinamente acreditamos ser bom e espiritual, mas prosseguimos sem discernir verdadeiramente a mente ou a vontade do Senhor para aquela situação. Consequentemente, uma sensação de vazio frequentemente se segue, deixando-nos insatisfeitos apesar de nossas melhores intenções. É somente quando nos alinhamos genuinamente e seguimos a direção do Senhor que alcançamos satisfação profunda e duradoura.

Para ilustrar isso, imagine um cenário onde um irmão observa outro irmão começando a se desviar do caminho correto, movendo-se em direção a um que poderia levar à corrupção espiritual. Repetidamente, um fardo, uma forte convicção, surgiu dentro dele de que deveria apontar clara e diretamente este desvio preocupante. No entanto, impulsionado por um desejo de ser percebido como um cristão gentil, ele decidiu abordar o irmão desviado com um rosto sorridente e oferecer apenas algumas palavras brandas de exortação. Surpreendentemente, depois de ter "descarregado seu fardo" desta maneira gentil, ele sentiu uma profunda sensação de vazio. De um ponto de vista humano, sua abordagem pode ter parecido bem-sucedida; sua atitude foi gentil e inofensiva exteriormente. No entanto, em vez de se sentir espiritualmente nutrido e fortalecido, ele sentiu uma profunda fome interior.

Apesar de nossas melhores intenções, é somente quando nos alinhamos genuinamente e seguimos a direção do Senhor que alcançamos satisfação profunda e duradoura.

Esta condição perturbadora persistiu por um tempo. Reconhecendo que algo estava fundamentalmente errado, ele buscou sinceramente o Senhor, pedindo iluminação e revelação sobre a verdadeira causa de seu esgotamento espiritual. Um dia, ele orou com sincera rendição: "Senhor, o que quer que Tu queiras que eu faça, eu o farei de acordo, sem reservas." O Senhor ouviu graciosamente sua oração e lhe mostrou claramente o caminho que deveria seguir. Pouco tempo depois, o irmão desviado inesperadamente veio vê-lo novamente. Desta vez, guiado pela mente do Senhor, o primeiro irmão o repreendeu com força e diretamente, falando com uma firmeza que era contrária ao seu temperamento natural. Historicamente, sua disposição natural significava que ele sofreria por dias sempre que proferisse qualquer palavra forte como aquela, sentindo o peso de suas próprias ações. Nesta ocasião, no entanto, ocorreu uma transformação notável: quanto mais forte ele falava, mais profundamente ele tocava o Senhor! A unção espiritual era evidente. Como resultado, depois de ter entregue esta forte repreensão, ele não sentiu necessidade, como era tipicamente o caso antes, de confessar qualquer pecado ou arrependimento; em vez disso, ele foi preenchido com louvor ao Senhor. Ele se sentiu como se tivesse participado de uma refeição espiritual completa e satisfatória.

Agora, é crucial esclarecer que esta instância não implica que devamos repreender as pessoas casualmente, descuidadamente ou em nossa própria raiva carnal; tais ações seriam, sem dúvida, erradas e contraproducentes. O significado deste exemplo reside unicamente em demonstrar que, se empreendermos qualquer ação, mesmo uma difícil, de acordo com a mente e a direção do Senhor, seremos alimentados interiormente, nutridos e, portanto, espiritualmente fortalecidos.

Deste exemplo, descobrimos um fato importante e libertador: que o "bem" que se pode realizar apenas por sua própria força natural, sua vontade humana ou sua gentileza inata, não é verdadeiro alimento espiritual. Você pode concluir intelectualmente que seria melhor ser mais gentil ou contundente em uma determinada situação, mas a experiência espiritual nos diz repetidamente que, mesmo que você aja de maneira gentil ou contundente a partir de seu homem exterior—seu eu natural—esta ação, por mais louvável que seja na aparência, não pode fornecer nutrição espiritual genuína. A nutrição verdadeira e duradoura e a satisfação profunda vêm apenas quando o próprio Senhor se move em você e você, por sua vez, se move em completa concordância com Sua vontade divina. Ao tocar verdadeiramente em Sua vida, você recebe alimento espiritual; ao tocar genuinamente no Senhor, você é profunda e completamente satisfeito.

Cristo é a Luz da Vida

O Senhor não se refere a Si mesmo apenas como "o pão da vida"; Ele também afirma poderosamente: "Eu sou a luz da vida." Pense assim: o pão tem tudo a ver com satisfazer nossa fome e prover sustento, enquanto a luz é essencial para vermos claramente e navegarmos em nosso ambiente. Assim como a satisfação nos dá a energia e a força para seguir em frente, ver claramente impacta diretamente a maneira como andamos pela vida. Já exploramos o significado profundo de Cristo como o pão da vida, e agora vamos nos aprofundar no que significa para Ele ser a luz da vida.

É crucial entender, desde o início, que esta "luz da vida" não se trata simplesmente de ter um vasto conhecimento da Bíblia. É claro que todo cristão sabe da importância de ler e estudar diligentemente suas Escrituras. No entanto, se abordarmos a

Bíblia meramente como uma fonte de conhecimento intelectual ou um livro didático de teologia, é exatamente isso que obteremos: apenas informação. Podemos nos tornar incrivelmente familiarizados com várias doutrinas bíblicas, até mesmo as corretas, mas elas permanecem apenas palavras em uma página, sem nos transformar verdadeiramente. Considere a época em que Jesus nasceu em Belém; muitos sacerdotes e escribas eram profundamente versados nos livros proféticos, mas falharam em reconhecer o próprio Cristo que aquelas profecias anunciavam. Hoje, com o Novo Testamento adicionado ao Velho, ainda é totalmente possível que as pessoas memorizem cada letra da Bíblia e, no entanto, não conheçam genuinamente a Cristo de uma maneira viva e pessoal. Certamente não estamos sugerindo que ler as Escrituras seja desnecessário; pelo contrário, estamos enfatizando que é possível obter muito conhecimento da Palavra sem nunca ter um encontro verdadeiro com o próprio Cristo através dela.

Na época de Cristo, muitos líderes religiosos, sacerdotes e escribas possuíam o que poderia ser descrito como um "conhecimento morto"—tinham entendimento intelectual, mas careciam de um relacionamento vivo e vibrante com o Senhor.

Infelizmente, muitas pessoas hoje ainda cometem o erro de igualar o mero conhecimento, a doutrina, a teologia ou o ensino com a verdadeira luz da vida. Alguns podem até alegar ter sido "iluminados", mas o que percebem como luz pode ser apenas uma interpretação particular de uma passagem da Escritura ou um ensinamento específico sobre a Bíblia. A luz real, no entanto, é muito mais do que apenas conhecimento ou percepção intelectual. É ninguém menos que o próprio Senhor Jesus Cristo. Ele declara enfaticamente: "Eu sou a luz da vida", significando que Ele é a fonte viva e iluminadora que nos guia, e não apenas uma coleção de fatos ou teorias. Esta luz nos capacita a ver verdades espirituais, a entender a vontade de Deus e a andar em Seus caminhos com clareza e propósito, muito além do que qualquer quantidade de estudo acadêmico por si só pode proporcionar. Na época de Cristo, muitos líderes religiosos, sacerdotes e escribas possuíam o que poderia ser descrito como um "conhecimento morto"—tinham entendimento intelectual, mas careciam de um relacionamento vivo e vibrante com o Senhor.

Nossa experiência como crentes é que o que percebemos genuinamente na luz da vida é frequentemente algo tão profundo e transformador que lutamos para colocar em palavras. Pode parecer estranho que possamos "ver" algo tão claramente, mas nos encontrarmos incapazes de articulá-lo completamente. Considere como exemplo a história de uma pessoa a quem perguntaram se ela era salva. Sua resposta simples, mas poderosa, foi: "Sim, eu sou salvo, mas não sei como explicar isso. Mas eu sei que estou salvo. Se você acredita que estou salvo, eu estou salvo; mesmo que você não acredite que eu estou salvo, eu ainda estou salvo." Suas palavras ressoaram com autenticidade. Ela havia experimentado uma transformação espiritual genuína, um profundo saber interior, mas a estrutura intelectual para explicar a salvação não estava imediatamente disponível para ela. Esta é frequentemente a nossa experiência: sabemos que sabemos porque vimos isso na luz. As palavras para isso podem nunca vir.

Então, qual é exatamente a profunda diferença entre ver esta luz e não vê-la? Que tipo de transformação radical ocorre em nós quando realmente a encontramos? A distinção é imensa, verdadeiramente monumental. Se vimos genuinamente esta luz divina, o efeito imediato e muitas vezes avassalador é que somos humilhados; nós "caímos por terra", por assim dizer. Isso ocorre porque esta luz não apenas ilumina nosso entendimento, mas também tem um efeito de "aniquilação" sobre nosso orgulho, nossa autossuficiência e nossas velhas maneiras de pensar. Pense na dramática conversão do Apóstolo Paulo no caminho para Damasco. Antes daquele poderoso encontro com a luz de Cristo, teria sido incrivelmente difícil humilhá-lo ou fazê-lo ceder. No entanto, assim que ele foi atingido por aquela luz intensa, foi instantaneamente lançado ao chão, totalmente abalado por seu poder.

Alguns indivíduos, em seu desejo sincero por crescimento espiritual, podem tentar se forçar à humildade. Suas palavras podem soar humildes, seus modos podem parecer modestos, mas este tipo de humildade autoimposta é incrivelmente exaustivo—tanto para eles quanto para aqueles ao seu redor. É como uma criança pequena tentando aprender todas as palavras de um grande dicionário: mesmo que o livro não seja fisicamente pesado, o mero esforço exigido esgota a força da criança. Quão incrivelmente difícil é para o coração orgulhoso se tornar genuinamente humilde! Quão desafiador é para nós descermos do "trono do orgulho" que frequentemente construímos para nós mesmos! Mas quando a luz pura e não adulterada do Senhor realmente brilha em nossas vidas, somos instantaneamente derrubados de nosso pedestal. Podemos não compreender intelectualmente *como* isso acontece, mas instintivamente entendemos que esta luz divina inerentemente nos leva a um lugar de profunda humildade e dependência de Deus. Ela elimina nossa autoconfiança e expõe a verdadeira condição de nossos corações, deixando-nos com nada além de uma profunda consciência de Sua majestade e de nossa necessidade d'Ele.

Podemos não compreender intelectualmente como isso acontece, mas instintivamente entendemos que a luz do Senhor inerentemente nos leva a um lugar de profunda humildade e dependência de Deus.

A doutrina, em si mesma, não causa inerentemente tropeço ou queda em ninguém. Alguém pode diligentemente ouvir inúmeras mensagens, até mesmo memorizando-as, mas seu ser interior permanece inalterado. Podem abordar uma mensagem profunda que deveria agitar suas emoções até as lágrimas, ou uma palavra poderosa destinada a quebrar sua vida egocêntrica, como nada mais do que um ritual semanal. Em tais tristes instâncias, a doutrina, o ensino e até mesmo a própria Palavra de Deus se tornam meras "coisas"—conceitos intelectuais desprovidos de vitalidade espiritual. Estes são essencialmente mortos; não há luz genuína irradiando deles para provocar a verdadeira transformação.

Esta luz divina é incrivelmente potente e rigorosa. Ela possui o poder de realizar o que o esforço humano sozinho não consegue. O que a doutrina intelectual falha em alcançar, o que a ajuda bem-intencionada de outros não pode trazer, e o que nossos próprios esforços extenuantes ficam aquém, esta luz pode realizar isso imediata e milagrosamente. Podemos nos perceber como duros de coração ou resistentes à mudança, mas quando a luz do Senhor brilha sobre nós, somos sobrenaturalmente amolecidos e maleáveis. Pense em João, que, ao encontrar esta luz, ficou "como morto" (Apocalipse 1:17); Daniel teve uma experiência semelhante. Ninguém é verdadeiramente capaz de contemplar o rosto glorioso do Senhor sem ser humilhado, sem cair em temor e reverência. É incrivelmente difícil para nossa natureza humana orgulhosa "morrer" para o eu, e é um desafio monumental para nós abraçarmos genuinamente a humildade. No entanto, assim que esta luz divina brilha, estas transformações aparentemente impossíveis ocorrem sem esforço. A luz que emana do Senhor carrega um "poder aniquilador." Ela leva as pessoas aos seus joelhos, não de forma destrutiva, mas de uma maneira que desmonta sua autossuficiência e as abre para a graça transformadora de Deus.

O próprio Senhor Jesus é a luz. Consequentemente, qualquer pessoa que realmente O encontra é profundamente afetada, muitas vezes sentindo-se subjugada e humilhada, como se tivesse sido levada à beira da morte espiritual. Muitos indivíduos possuem um caráter naturalmente forte e inflexível; nunca foram verdadeiramente quebrantados ou amolecidos pelo Senhor, e nem eles nem mais ninguém parece ser capaz de lidar com sua teimosia. No entanto, quando a luz radiante do Senhor brilha sobre eles, algo notável acontece. Assim que percebem esta luz, sua dura casca exterior começa a rachar, e eles se tornam "vasos quebrados", prontos para serem remodelados por Deus. Uma pessoa que vê genuinamente o Senhor é inegavelmente enfraquecida em sua autoconfiança e profundamente humilhada. É como se sua velha maneira de viver se tornasse impossível após contemplar Sua glória. Isto, em seu poder transformador, é o que queremos dizer com "luz".

A perspectiva de Davi sobre o Senhor era que Ele é quem traz luz para sua escuridão. O ponto-chave na vida de Davi não era seu brilho, mas sim sua dependência. "Porque tu acenderás a minha candeia; o Senhor meu Deus iluminará as minhas trevas." (Salmos 18:28).

O primeiro e mais profundo efeito desta luz divina é "aniquilar"—desmontar nossa autossuficiência e orgulho. Não creia erroneamente que a luz vem unicamente para nos permitir ver de forma clara. Não é bem assim. Quando esta luz poderosa realmente brilha sobre nós, seu impacto inicial é muitas vezes "cegar" nossos olhos naturais, ou pelo menos nos deixar atordoados. Embora ela de fato nos faça ver, este é um efeito subsequente, seguindo a humilhação inicial. A luz primeiro nos subjuga e nos prostra antes que realmente nos capacite a perceber as realidades espirituais com clareza. Qualquer coisa que digamos que recebemos do Senhor que não nos leva aos joelhos, que não nos humilha profundamente, não é a verdadeira luz de Cristo. Lembre-se da experiência de Paulo: quando ele viu a luz, foi imediatamente lançado ao chão e permaneceu cego por três dias. Portanto, durante nosso encontro inicial com esta luz, é provável que fiquemos atordoados, desorientados e profundamente impactados. No momento em que alguém que estava habitando na escuridão espiritual contempla esta luz, encontrará sua velha maneira de ver, e na verdade sua velha maneira de ser, completamente abalada.

Que Deus tenha misericórdia daqueles que estão tão profundamente enraizados na justiça própria e na presunção. Tais indivíduos, infelizmente, nunca encontraram verdadeiramente o poder iluminador da luz divina; tudo o que possuem são meras doutrinas e conhecimento intelectual. Se tivessem visto verdadeiramente a luz genuína, sua confissão imediata e sincera seria: "Ó Senhor, o que é que eu sei? Nada. Eu não sei absolutamente nada por mim mesmo!" Isso ilustra um princípio espiritual profundo: quanto maior a revelação da luz de Deus, mais profunda é a nossa consciência da nossa própria cegueira espiritual; quanto mais forte a luz brilha, mais severo é o "golpe" que ela desfere em nosso orgulho e autossuficiência.

É vital entender que a luz não é um conceito abstrato; é algo incrivelmente substancial e real. O próprio Senhor Jesus é essa luz. Com Ele habitando entre nós e em nós, temos a verdadeira luz em nosso meio.

Esta luz divina nos humilhará e nos levará aos nossos joelhos *antes* que realmente nos capacite a ver com clareza espiritual. Se não fomos profundamente atingidos, humilhados, atordoados e, em última análise, reduzidos a um estado de total dependência de Deus, isso serve como prova inegável de que ainda estamos habitando na escuridão espiritual, não possuindo luz verdadeira. Que o Senhor, em Sua infinita misericórdia, faça Sua luz brilhar sobre nós de forma tão poderosa que elimine nossa autoconfiança, impedindo-nos de sequer ousar confiar em nosso próprio conhecimento limitado e julgamento falho mais uma vez. Ah, que possamos vir a Ele com o coração bem aberto, declarando: "Senhor, Tu és a luz. Ao ver-Te, agora percebo que tudo o que eu considerava 'verdade' ou 'entendimento' no passado eram meras 'coisas'—conceitos abstratos, e não a realidade viva de Tua presença."

É vital entender que a luz não é um conceito abstrato; é algo incrivelmente substancial e real. O próprio Senhor Jesus *é* essa luz. Com Ele habitando entre nós e em nós, temos a verdadeira luz em nosso meio. É realmente lamentável quantos aspectos da vida dos crentes permanecem puramente teóricos. Eles ouviram inúmeros ensinamentos e conceitos abstratos que, embora talvez intelectualmente estimulantes, oferecem muito pouca ajuda prática ou poder transformador em suas vidas diárias.

Por que será que, depois de alguns dias, as verdades profundas de Deus que ouvimos parecem perder seu poder, tornando-se tão fracas que não nos tocam ou transformam profundamente? Não há outra razão senão esta: tornou-se muita doutrina, muito conhecimento teológico, sem a presença viva de Cristo! Consideremos a santidade, por exemplo. Depois de ouvir muitas discussões sobre o conceito de santidade, posso decidir mergulhar profundamente na doutrina da santidade. Posso pesquisar meticulosamente o Novo Testamento e encontrar mais de duzentos versículos sobre o assunto. Eu memorizo cada um e os organizo cuidadosamente em uma ordem sistemática. Apesar de todo esse esforço intelectual, eu ainda não *sei* o que é a santidade; e provavelmente sentirei um profundo vazio interior. Este sentimento de vazio espiritual persistirá porque a santidade não é um conhecimento desincorporado. Mas se um dia eu encontrar alguém que genuinamente incorporou a santidade, meus olhos espirituais se abrirão para realmente *ver* o que é a santidade, porque eu encontrei uma pessoa que era santa. A luz deste tipo de revelação é avassaladora, quase terrível em sua intensidade, porque a luz me atravessará. Isso pode me causar imensa dor interior, não oferecendo escapatória de sua verdade. Isso me mostrou inequivocamente o que a santidade realmente é. Eu poderia dizer então que o Senhor trouxe luz para a minha escuridão (falta de santidade neste caso) e eu pude ver claramente.

Nós precisamos desesperadamente reconhecer que somente o Deus vivo pode verdadeiramente gerar pessoas vivas. Devemos orar sinceramente para que Deus seja misericordioso conosco, permitindo-nos cada vez mais ver que todas as "coisas"—todos os conceitos espirituais, práticas e até mesmo dons, se separados de Cristo—são, em última análise, mortos. Só o Senhor é quem é vivo, vibrante e eternamente ativo. Mesmo os aspectos mais atraentes e aparentemente espirituais do Cristianismo, se existirem fora de uma conexão viva com Cristo, são apenas formas sem vida. Devemos permitir que o próprio Senhor *seja* esta coisa ou aquela coisa para nós. Então, e somente então, isso se torna verdadeiramente vivo—vivo tanto em nós quanto naqueles que recebem de nós. Que o Senhor seja gracioso conosco, levando-nos a um lugar de profunda humildade diante d'Ele, onde possamos realmente conhecê-Lo de uma maneira que transcenda o mero entendimento intelectual.

"O povo que andava em trevas, viu uma grande luz, e sobre os que habitavam na região da sombra da morte resplandeceu a luz." (Isaías 9:2).

Senhor meu Deus, hoje estamos com corações transbordando em celebração pela gloriosa verdade do Teu Filho, Jesus Cristo, que é o Pão da nossa Vida e a Luz do nosso Mundo! Nós celebramos que Tu nos deste nada menos que o próprio Cristo, e que Ele não é apenas um provedor, mas a própria essência de tudo o que necessitamos.

Nós celebramos que Jesus declara: "Eu sou o pão da vida." Nós não nos esforçamos mais para encontrar nutrição espiritual ou buscar satisfação temporária, pois O recebemos como a essência que sustenta nossa vida e que satisfaz completamente as nossas almas. Nós celebramos que Ele é o nosso sustento constante e diário, e que vir a Ele significa que nunca teremos fome, e crer Nele significa que nunca mais teremos sede.

Nós celebramos que Jesus também proclama: "Eu sou a luz da vida." Nós nos regozijamos por Ele não ser apenas capaz de nos dar luz, mas por ser a própria fonte e essência de toda luz e verdade divinas. Nós celebramos que, ao segui-Lo, somos eternamente libertados de andar em trevas e agora temos a Luz eterna da vida brilhando dentro de nós.

Nós celebramos que Tu abriste nossos olhos espirituais para vermos que Cristo é o nosso Tudo. Nós Te agradecemos por transformar nossa jornada espiritual de um esforço religioso em simplesmente receber e desfrutar de um relacionamento com a Pessoa que é o tudo.

Oramos no nome poderoso de Jesus, amém!

6

Tudo Gira em Torno de uma Pessoa

Tudo gira em torno de uma Pessoa. Você pode se perguntar por que focamos tanto neste ponto essencial, mas compreendê-lo é a diferença entre um Cristianismo Vivo e próspero e um outro que é desgastante e cheio de fórmulas. A diferença entre essas duas abordagens é imensa, quase incalculável. Uma é vibrante, espiritual e divina, fluindo do coração de Deus; a outra é, muitas vezes, apenas um sistema de esforço e invenção criado por nós humanos. Quando você estuda a Bíblia com um coração aberto, você descobrirá esta verdade profunda: toda a narrativa gira em torno de uma única e gloriosa Pessoa, e não de uma coleção de 'coisas' espirituais fragmentadas ou conceitos abstratos. Essa Pessoa é o Senhor Jesus Cristo, e n'Ele, você tem o quadro completo.

Um grande desafio para os crentes de hoje é que sua visão de fé pode ser fragmentada, como uma colcha de retalhos de pedaços separados. Frequentemente, ouvimos uma vida cristã ser descrita por suas partes: "Eu recebi um pouco de graça", "Eu tenho esse dom espiritual", "Estou trabalhando na minha paciência", ou "Ela tem uma grande medida de humildade". Isso se torna o que é frequentemente *chamado* de Cristianismo. Mas, é isso? Não. O Cristianismo é o Próprio Cristo. Não é uma recompensa a ser conquistada, nem é meramente uma lista de dons que Cristo *me* dá. O Cristianismo é nada menos que a presença dinâmica e pessoal de Cristo em minha vida.

Você consegue ver a distinção crucial, que muda a forma de viver? Estes são dois caminhos inteiramente diferentes. O Cristianismo não é sobre receber um item isolado *de* Cristo; é sobre Cristo se dando a mim completamente e sem reservas. A luta em nossos dias é que muitos crentes tratam o Cristianismo como uma dádiva espiritual. Pensamos: "Quando eu era um pecador, Cristo me deu Sua misericórdia. Agora que sou cristão, Ele me dá paciência, depois me dá humildade, depois me dá mansidão", e assim por diante, como se essas fossem virtudes separadas a serem colecionadas. Mas a verdade é muito mais gloriosa e simples.

A Natureza Pessoal da Fé

Diante de Deus, não se trata de Ele nos *conceder* qualidades espirituais, mas de Deus nos dar o Próprio Cristo. Ele não apenas lhe concedeu humildade, paciência ou mansidão como traços separados; Ele lhe concedeu a totalidade de Cristo. É o Senhor Jesus vivo quem se torna a sua humildade, a sua paciência e a sua mansidão. Esta é a própria essência do que é verdadeiramente chamado de Cristianismo.

É vital reconhecer que não há absolutamente nada impessoal na vida cristã. Cada elemento da sua caminhada com Deus é pessoal porque a Pessoa envolvida é Cristo. Dito de outra forma, vamos reformular aqueles termos espirituais que frequentemente tratamos como "coisas":

- A sua Paciência não é uma *coisa*; a sua paciência é uma Pessoa.
- A sua Santificação não é uma *experiência* ou um processo; a sua santificação é um Homem.
- A sua Justificação não é uma declaração *abstrata*; a sua justificação é uma Personalidade.
- A sua Justiça não é um *comportamento* perfeito; a sua justiça é um Ser.

Quando somos salvos e libertos, não obtemos uma lista de itens; a nossa redenção, libertação, paciência, humildade e amor são todos o Próprio Senhor—eles não são coisas. Esta é a realidade genuína e libertadora do Cristianismo. Na vida de um verdadeiro crente, Cristo já é a resposta que inclui tudo, e não precisamos esperar por um dia futuro para experimentar esta plenitude.

Muitas pessoas naturalmente perguntam: *Como é possível dizer que Cristo é tudo?* A resposta é simples: se você realmente compreendeu o cerne relacional de um Cristianismo vivo, você reconhecerá sem esforço que Cristo é tudo. Não é que Ele *dá* todas as coisas; é que Ele *é* todas as coisas.

Uma luta comum e uma grande fonte de derrota para os filhos de Deus é esta confusão. Eles estão focados em adquirir a dádiva em vez de abraçar Aquele que a *dá*. Eles buscam itens espirituais fragmentados, mas perdem o Cristo de Deus por completo. Eles possuem objetos e coisas (uma regra, uma prática, uma doutrina), mas não a Pessoa que é suficiente para todas as coisas. Obter esta única e vital perspectiva—de que Cristo é tudo—é a solução que resolve todos os outros problemas na vida espiritual.

Toda a narrativa da Bíblia gira em torno de uma única e gloriosa Pessoa, não de uma coleção de conceitos abstratos. Essa Pessoa é o Senhor Jesus Cristo, e n'Ele, você tem o quadro completo.

Considere o momento em que você foi salvo. Você ouviu a gloriosa mensagem de João 3:16, que diz: "Porque Deus amou o mundo de tal maneira que deu o seu Filho unigênito, para que todo aquele que nele crê não pereça, mas tenha a vida eterna." Você sentiu a sua necessidade de salvação e orou sinceramente. Mas com que frequência os crentes ainda vão a Deus e imploram: "Senhor, Tu és o meu Salvador, mas será que pode *também* me dar a salvação?" Parece tolice pedir pelo produto quando você tem a Fonte, como se o Próprio Salvador não fosse suficiente. No entanto, muitos ainda fazem isso de muitas maneiras.

O evangelho que pregamos é que Deus nos deu o Salvador. A verdade que devemos agarrar na oração é esta: Deus tem um

Filho, e este Filho é a sua salvação. Ao possuir o Salvador, você já possui a salvação. Por que implorar pelo segundo quando você tem o primeiro? É o ápice da libertação perceber que, desde que você abraçou o Salvador, você tem tudo.

Esta é a razão pela qual Deus revela que o próprio nome de Cristo é "EU SOU." Este nome não é apenas uma descrição do Seu poder; é a promessa máxima da Sua completude. Ele não é apenas Aquele que *irá* prover; Ele é o Autoexistente, o Todo Suficiente para todas as Coisas, Ele é a resposta para toda e qualquer necessidade que você jamais enfrentará. Somos convidados, e até mesmo impelidos, a entender e experimentar a plenitude libertadora deste nome abençoado em nossa caminhada diária.

O Alimento Vivo

O Senhor Jesus faz uma declaração notável no Evangelho de João: "Eu sou o pão da vida." Contudo, em nossa fome humana, frequentemente perdemos o significado desta declaração. Nós nos aproximamos d'Ele pedindo por "pão", tratando-o como uma mercadoria simples ou um item em uma lista de compras espiritual. Sentimos a dor profunda e o vazio por dentro e sinceramente imploramos a Deus que nos dê algo para preenchê-lo, algum tipo de alimento, se for da Sua vontade.

É uma descoberta verdadeiramente surpreendente perceber que, muitas vezes, aqueles que estão apenas implorando pelo "pão" impessoal nunca o recebem na forma que esperam e, como resultado, sua fome mais profunda persiste. Isso levanta uma questão natural: as promessas de Deus são, de alguma forma, falhas? A Escritura não nos assegura que "Pois fartou a alma sedenta, e encheu de bens a alma faminta" (Salmos 107:9) e que "Encheu de bens os famintos, e despediu vazios os ricos" (Lucas 1:53)? Absolutamente, a Palavra de Deus é verdadeira!

A chave poderosa reside em entender *o que* são verdadeiramente esses "bens". A verdade profunda que nos satisfaz completamente diante de Deus não é um conceito abstrato ou uma mera provisão física; é o Próprio Cristo.

Com que frequência sentimos esse vazio espiritual, acreditando que Deus tem o suprimento e esperando que algum "alimento" tangível se materialize de nossa oração? Frequentemente não sabemos o mecanismo exato para receber este alimento. Tudo o que realmente precisamos fazer é continuar nos achegando ao Senhor, confiando e aceitando mais d'Ele, e simplesmente desfrutando da Sua presença.

A bela surpresa é esta: mesmo quando o "alimento" específico que imaginamos não aparece, nos encontramos profunda e totalmente satisfeitos. Não obtemos o item que pedimos mentalmente, mas a nossa proximidade com o Senhor proporciona uma satisfação sobrenatural. Somos satisfeitos por crermos e recebermos *totalmente a Ele*.

Há uma razão transformadora e profunda para a minha constante alegria e louvores sem fim a Deus: a minha justiça não é um conjunto de regras, um registro do meu próprio desempenho, ou um sentimento passageiro. É uma Pessoa viva e que respira o mesmo ar: o Próprio Senhor Jesus Cristo. Esta verdade é incrivelmente libertadora e fundamental para a nossa fé!

Pense na maravilha disso: porque a minha justiça é o Senhor Jesus, isso significa que eu não apenas *possuo* uma boa posição diante de Deus; eu tenho um *relacionamento* dinâmico com a minha posição. Eu posso realmente falar com a minha justiça! Eu posso louvá-lO, dar-Lhe glória e agradecer-Lhe porque Ele é a minha própria perfeição, dada gratuitamente. Você pode parar e se perguntar: "Como você pode louvar a sua justiça?" Eu posso fazer isso todos os dias, porque a minha justiça não é um conceito abstrato ou uma "coisa" que eu ganhei—é a Pessoa gloriosa de Cristo, Aquele que é tudo.

Este mesmo princípio se aplica à minha santidade, que está igualmente fora do âmbito do meu frágil comportamento. Minha santidade não é o resultado do meu esforço extenuante ou de uma exibição impressionante de comportamento disciplinado. Eu posso louvar a minha santidade, mas com certeza *não* estou louvando a minha própria conduta! Minhas próprias ações frequentemente ficam aquém, e eu detesto as deficiências da minha velha natureza. Mas eu posso gritar louvores à minha santidade porque a minha santidade também é o meu Senhor. Ele habita em mim, e a Sua vida perfeita e pura é a santidade que eu celebro.

Esta é a distinção gloriosa e radical da vida cristã. Estamos contrastando duas realidades totalmente opostas: de um lado, há uma coisa inanimada—o nosso fraco esforço humano, um conjunto de doutrinas, ou uma lista de bons comportamentos. Do outro lado está o Senhor—uma Pessoa vibrante, viva e plenamente suficiente. Quando Cristo é a nossa Justiça e Santidade, tudo flui com vida divina e ausência de esforço, dando-nos uma confiança inabalável e uma fonte infinita de louvor. Não se trata de *cumprir* a vida cristã; trata-se de *contemplar* e *receber* Aquele que é tudo para nós.

O Processo de Deus de Refinar e Reconstruir

É um fato surpreendentemente comum e muitas vezes desconcertante da vida espiritual: muitos de nós descobrimos que, depois de anos — até mesmo décadas — de sermos cristãos, lutamos com as mesmas coisas que pareciam dominar facilmente no início. Ouvimos de outros crentes como, logo no começo, eles eram naturalmente capazes de ser pacientes, rápidos em perdoar e consistentes na oração. Conseguiriam lidar com situações difíceis na escola, em casa ou no trabalho com uma quantidade surpreendente de graça. Mas e agora? Agora, eles confessam que simplesmente não conseguem sustentar isso. Mesmo que consigam evitar um desabafo completo, o pensamento interior de ressentimento ou até mesmo o desejo de retaliação pode ser uma luta constante. Essas histórias estão por toda parte. É desanimador descobrir que a humildade, a paciência, a mansidão, o amor e o zelo que antes pareciam tão prontamente disponíveis agora são difíceis de acessar ou simplesmente desapareceram.

Se você já passou por isso, anime-se—este declínio inesperado na sua bondade natural é frequentemente um sinal da obra mais profunda e gloriosa de Deus em sua vida.

Aqui está uma verdade vital para você e eu: Deus deve remover gentilmente, mas com firmeza, toda *coisa* em nós que não é Cristo.

Quando viemos pela primeira vez ao Senhor, reconhecemos uma necessidade, talvez de amor em um relacionamento difícil. Então, pedimos a Deus por amor e, em certo sentido, Ele graciosamente nos deu um "kit inicial"—uma medida de amor para nos ajudar a começar. Naquele momento, o amor era como um presente externo, um *objeto* que possuíamos. Mas aqui está o ponto crucial: o desejo final de Deus não é que você simplesmente tenha uma *sacola de amor* para sempre. Ele está determinado a fazer da Pessoa de Cristo o seu amor. E para conseguir isso, Ele tem que, eventualmente, permitir que aquela "coisa" ou "objeto" inicial, próprio seu, chamado amor seja tirado.

O mesmo padrão se aplica a cada virtude espiritual. Se você era naturalmente de temperamento explosivo antes da salvação, você pode ter visto inicialmente a paciência como um dom singular, uma "salvação em si" que consertaria tudo. Isso pode ter sustentado você por alguns anos, mas, eventualmente, "esmoreceu". Seu esforço próprio e a graça inicial *como uma dádiva* provaram ser temporários.

Deus realiza esta obra contínua—este processo profundo de remover e substituir—na vida de todos os Seus filhos. Ele tira não apenas as distrações do mundo, mas, mais profundamente, as coisas espirituais nas quais nos apoiamos. Antes de sermos salvos, as coisas deste mundo naturalmente tomavam o lugar que pertence a Cristo. Agora que somos salvos, podemos ser tentados a substituir esse foco mundano por coisas espirituais— boas qualidades, experiências ou ministérios—que também sutilmente começam a ocupar o lugar central de Cristo.

Mas Deus está em uma missão para nos mostrar uma nova realidade de tirar o fôlego: "Cristo é o meu tudo."

Ele remove a sua paciência própria, o seu amor vindo de si mesmo, o seu poder humano, a sua mansidão natural e a sua humildade autoproduzida. Ele remove tudo isso para que a sua vida não seja mais sustentada por uma coleção de *coisas* boas, mas sim por uma Pessoa viva. Somos pacientes, não porque recebemos um *poder* para sermos pacientes, mas porque recebemos uma Pessoa—Cristo—que é a própria paciência. Esta é a verdade para a humildade, mansidão e todas as outras virtudes: não é um poder, mas uma Pessoa.

Isto explica por que Deus se engaja em um processo contínuo de destruir e construir. Ele está diariamente desmantelando a nossa confiança em *coisas* para que possa diariamente edificar Cristo em nossa experiência. No passado, você pode ter orado por um dom ou um poder para resolver um problema específico, como impaciência ou falta de humildade. Você sentiu que um problema foi resolvido, apenas para passar para o próximo, tentando resolver problemas fracionados um por um.

Aqui está uma verdade vital para você e eu: Deus deve remover gentilmente, mas com firmeza, toda coisa em nós que não é Cristo.

A notícia mais animadora é que Deus está simplificando toda a sua vida espiritual. Ele está tirando todas aquelas "coisas" separadas para que possa lhe dar uma Pessoa onipresente que é simultaneamente a sua humildade, a sua paciência, a sua mansidão e o seu amor. Cristo é tudo, e esta é a verdadeira essência de um Cristianismo vibrante. Deus trabalha incansavelmente até que não apenas nossos corações, mas todo o universo confesse que Cristo é, de fato, tudo. Hoje, o Seu maior desejo é estabelecer e tornar realidade em você esta confissão profunda: Cristo é tudo.

Pense na profunda diferença que isso faz em como nos relacionamos com os outros. Ao ministrar a alguém que está lutando, podemos instintivamente exortá-lo: "Você agiu sem amor, deve tentar demonstrar mais amor por eles da próxima vez." Se ele for bem-sucedido através de pura força de vontade, ele alcançou o amor como uma mera *coisa*, um ajuste comportamental. Isso resulta no que podemos chamar de Cristianismo comportamental—uma vida que consiste em exibir certos comportamentos corretos através do esforço humano: é o homem que está trabalhando, pedindo, esperando, crendo e sendo bem-sucedido em um ato exterior de amor. Neste cenário, o amor é apenas uma *marca de comportamento*.

Isto está a um universo de distância da experiência de Amar como Cristo. Quando o amor é Cristo, ele deixa de ser um comportamento forçado da vontade humana e se torna uma lei de vida espontânea. Não sou mais eu quem está trabalhando para amar; é Cristo quem ama através de mim. Que vida cristã verdadeiramente distinta e gloriosa é esta, livre da exaustão do esforço próprio!

"Já estou crucificado com Cristo; e vivo, não mais eu, mas Cristo vive em mim; e a vida que agora vivo na carne, vivo-a pela fé do Filho de Deus, o qual me amou, e se entregou a si mesmo por mim." (Gálatas 2:20)

É crucial perguntar a si mesmo: Quando você ajuda alguém, ela se vai equipada com uma nova *coisa* espiritual ou se vai com uma *revelação mais profunda de Cristo*? Muitos crentes sinceros ainda estão ocupados com "as coisas" no Cristianismo—as virtudes, os métodos, os dons—e ainda não conheceram Cristo como o magnífico tudo de Deus. A graça de Deus está ativamente em ação, removendo todos os substitutos para revelar a única fonte duradoura e vivificante: a Pessoa de

Jesus Cristo. Seu crescimento espiritual não é uma tarefa a ser realizada, mas uma Pessoa a ser continuamente descoberta.

O Mergulho Profundo: Experimentando Cristo como seu Tudo

Vamos explorar o que realmente significa ir além de simplesmente *saber sobre* Cristo para *conhecer* Cristo de forma genuína na realidade prática e a cada momento da sua vida. Isso não é uma teoria teológica; é uma transformação que toca a sua existência diária — os seus "afazeres e circunstâncias".

Conhecer Cristo nesse sentido mais profundo significa reconhecê-Lo como a própria essência de suas virtudes. Por exemplo, você deixa de se esforçar para ter paciência e descobre que Cristo é a sua paciência. Você não tenta mais forçar o amor; você percebe que Cristo é o seu amor. Outros podem descobrir que Cristo se tornou a sua própria humildade. Este nível de conhecimento é o catalisador para uma mudança fundamental, dramática e libertadora na sua vida.

Quando esta revelação surge, você pode declarar com confiança que não existem mais "coisas" separadas no seu mundo espiritual. O seu mundo, até mesmo a sua caminhada cristã, é totalmente e belamente resumida em Cristo. Você não tem santidade fora d'Ele, e essa é a boa notícia. Isso não significa que você é profano; significa que a sua santidade não é mais um padrão pessoal que você se esforça para alcançar. Em vez disso, Cristo agora é a sua santidade. Esta compreensão imediata de que "Cristo é tudo" liberta você completamente do esforço exaustivo de manter coisas externas e geradas por si mesmo. Todo o caminho para a maturidade espiritual está envolto nesta única busca: um conhecimento vivo de Cristo, e não uma questão de pura força de vontade, pedidos intermináveis de oração por coisas, ou encorajamento externo.

Esta é uma verdade crucial para a nossa fé: a mudança duradoura nunca se inicia por mera exortação ou encorajamento. Embora palavras de incentivo possam motivar temporariamente uma pessoa ao esforço próprio, a verdadeira e eficaz transformação acontece quando Deus abre os seus olhos espirituais para conhecer Cristo. Os nossos esforços mais sinceros podem ser repetidos cem vezes sem resultado duradouro, até que vejamos que Cristo é a própria solução que estamos buscando.

Considere a luta diária com as virtudes cristãs. Muitos crentes conhecem Cristo como o seu Senhor que os justifica, mas ainda lutam com o medo diante de Deus porque não experimentaram Cristo como a sua justiça. Da mesma forma, muitos O conhecem como o Santificador, mas constantemente se sentem inadequados em santidade. Por quê? Eles buscam a santidade como uma "coisa" — uma meta a ser alcançada. Eles pedem ao Santificador que lhes dê poder para serem santos. Mas, ao confiarem nesse "poder", eles inevitavelmente atingem um muro, descobrindo a sua incapacidade pessoal de sustentá-lo.

A luta deles é superada e seus corações são libertos somente depois que Deus abre os seus olhos para verem que Cristo é a sua santidade — não o seu desejo sincero por santidade, e nem mesmo o poder para ser santo que Ele concede. Cristo se torna santidade neles. Esta é a profunda estabilidade e segurança da vida cristã: podemos perder o poder ou falhar em nossas ações, mas nunca podemos perder Cristo. A nossa santidade genuína está estabelecida, repousando inteiramente no que Ele é para nós, e não no que fazemos. Quando O conhecemos como tudo, os nossos problemas mais persistentes são resolvidos. A mensagem final é singular e poderosa: Cristo é tudo.

Aqui está um ponto comum de confusão: muitas pessoas conhecem Cristo como o seu Senhor, mas ainda não O reconhecem como tal em seus afazeres e circunstâncias. Frequentemente percebemos Cristo apenas em termos de Seus atos, o que pode ser visto nos títulos com "or":

- Salvador
- Redentor
- Santificador
- Justificador

Mas Deus deseja que O conheçamos na realidade mais profunda e mais sublime como nos títulos com "ão":

- Salvação
- Redenção
- Santificação
- Justificação

Conhecê-Lo como o "or" é um conhecimento fundamental; conhecê-Lo como o "ão" — a real essência da obra — é um conhecimento mais avançado e mais profundo.

As vidas espirituais de muitos crentes estão cheias de muitas "coisas" separadas. O dia em que finalmente vemos que "Ele é", e que cada uma de nossas necessidades espirituais foi consolidada em uma única e gloriosa Pessoa, é o dia em que o propósito eterno de Deus é realizado em nós. Enquanto a nossa santificação, redenção, regeneração, poder, graça e dons permanecerem como objetos separados que buscamos, estaremos na periferia do Cristianismo. Mas quando vemos que estes não são coisas, mas o próprio Senhor, nós realmente entramos no propósito eterno de Deus. Daquele momento em diante, é sempre Ele, nunca uma coleção de coisas.

As "coisas" que nos esforçamos para alcançar por nossa própria força estão, em um sentido espiritual, mortas. Uma vez que percebemos isso, essas mesmas "coisas" perdem o seu poder sobre nós e encontram a sua verdadeira realidade e vitalidade na Pessoa de Cristo. A minha regeneração, por exemplo, não é um conceito; ela tem uma Personalidade. Cristo, a quem eu possuo, é uma Pessoa, e não uma coisa. Toda virtude e bênção que eu tenho carrega a Sua personalidade porque o Senhor é tudo. Ele nos leva primeiro a conhecê-Lo, e depois nos leva mais adiante a conhecê-Lo como tudo o que precisamos. Nisto, somos verdadeiramente libertos do fardo da nossa própria vida de esforço e da busca incessante do mundo espiritual.

Podemos testemunhar que, em nosso viver diário, Ele é tudo.

- Se sou paciente hoje, não sou eu quem sou paciente, mas Aquele que vive em mim é paciente.
- Se eu amo, não é porque estou me esforçando ao máximo para amar — o poder não está em mim — mas porque há Um que ama em mim.
- Se eu perdoo, não é devido ao meu esforço, generosidade ou capacidade; é puramente devido Àquele que vive em mim e sempre perdoa. Ele é o meu perdão.
- Se sou humilde, não é porque estou reprimindo o orgulho ou forçando uma atitude humilde; é a Pessoa em mim quem Se humilha. Visto que Ele é a minha humildade, eu sou consequentemente humilde.

Esta é a bela lei da vida: Cristo Se tornando a nossa vida, bem como a essência de todas as nossas virtudes espirituais.

Portanto, peçamos todos sinceramente a Deus que abra os nossos olhos para que possamos ver verdadeiramente esta realidade monumental. Todos os nossos esforços humanos, métodos e "coisas" externas acabarão por desaparecer, mas o que permanece é eternamente Cristo. Que possamos viver esta incrível verdade todos os dias e deixar que Cristo seja tudo em nossos corações agora mesmo.

Pai amado,

Nós nos achegamos a Ti com humildade e gratidão, maravilhados com a profundidade da Tua provisão em Teu Filho, Jesus Cristo.

Reconhecemos que, muitas vezes, nos contentamos em conhecê-Lo apenas por Seus atos, como o Salvador que nos resgata e o Justificador que declara a nossa inocência. Mas hoje, com o coração aberto, buscamos ir além.

Pedimos-Te, Pai, que abras os nossos olhos espirituais para vermos a realidade monumental de que Cristo é muito mais do que Aquele que realiza uma obra: Ele é a própria obra.

Que possamos enxergar que Ele não é apenas o nosso Salvador, mas a nossa completa e definitiva Salvação. Ele não é apenas o nosso Justificador, mas a nossa eterna Justificação. Ele é, de fato, a nossa Santificação, a nossa Redenção, e a nossa Esperança.

Nós Te entregamos todos os nossos esforços humanos, os nossos métodos falhos e as "coisas" externas que buscamos incessantemente. Sabemos que tudo isso é passageiro e ineficaz. Ajuda-nos a viver com o descanso e a segurança de que só o que permanece é o Cristo eterno. Amém.

Vamos Orar !

7

A Cruz

A Chave de Viver pela Vida de Cristo

Vamos analisar o propósito da cruz com absoluta clareza e com uma perspectiva encorajadora. A Cruz de Cristo não é apenas a chave para a nossa salvação do pecado; ela é a chave operacional diária para toda a nossa vida espiritual. Podemos dizer claramente: Se você está vivendo a vida pela sua própria força — nas suas 'coisas' — você, na verdade, não precisa do poder da cruz. Mas se você está comprometido a viver pela Pessoa de Cristo, você abraçará a cruz diariamente.

A cruz é uma força que a tudo abrange. Sim, ela lida radicalmente com o nosso pecado, cortando tudo o que é abertamente mau. No entanto, em nossa jornada espiritual, ela vai mais fundo: ela inibe o nosso esforço humano. Ela foi planejada para frear as nossas ações próprias e controlar o nosso desejo natural de fazer, até mesmo o bem.

É aqui que muitos crentes sinceros se deparam com uma profunda dificuldade. Eles genuinamente querem fazer o bem, ser compassivos e servir aos outros. Contudo, eles não percebem que essa "bondade" de origem humana é apenas mais uma coisa — um produto espiritual da sua própria energia natural. Aos olhos de Deus, o importante, a única substância, é o próprio Cristo. Ele é a única coisa verdadeiramente boa, a fonte de toda a vida.

Pense nisto: Se Cristo, a própria Vida do seu espírito, permanece em silêncio, como podemos ousar agir por conta própria? Podemos facilmente começar a dar conselhos bem-intencionados ou oferecer um dilúvio de palavras de conforto, mas se Ele não nos impulsionou, devemos nos conter. Por quê? Porque quando operamos fora da Sua iniciativa, nos encontramos tocando a morte espiritual. É por isso que você pode ajudar pessoas, ganhar elogios pelo seu coração terno e, ainda assim, sentir instantaneamente um vazio, um cansaço e desânimo por dentro. O esforço foi genuíno, mas a fonte estava vazia.

Este é o poder mais profundo da Cruz: ela não apenas julga o nosso mal; ela julga a nossa bondade própria que é independente de Cristo. Qualquer bem que realizamos usando a nossa própria habilidade, força humana ou força de vontade religiosa não requer que a cruz seja eficaz. A cruz se torna essencial somente quando escolhemos recuar e permitir que o Senhor viva através de nós, fazendo d'Ele a fonte das nossas ações, da nossa sabedoria e do nosso tudo.

Temos que nos perguntar: Se Cristo não se move, como eu posso me mover? Esta é uma rendição diária. Precisamos orar por libertação da tirania das nossas próprias boas obras com a mesma paixão com que oramos por libertação dos nossos pecados. Para muitos, é surpreendentemente mais fácil ser liberto do pecado que é evidente, que é claramente condenado, do que ser liberto da nossa vida natural e egocêntrica. Por quê? Porque as nossas próprias "boas obras" não são rejeitadas pelo mundo, tornando-as muito mais difíceis de reconhecer e entregar. Mas o caminho para uma vida frutífera e sem esforço é deixar a cruz pôr um fim aos nossos esforços, para que a vida de Cristo possa começar a fluir.

Somente Cristo

Qual é a verdade fundamental e mais libertadora da nossa fé? É uma realidade que muitas vezes passa despercebida: no reino espiritual, não existe **nada além de Cristo**.

Frequentemente, buscamos o que chamamos de "virtudes espirituais" como se fossem "coisas" separadas e alcançáveis que podemos colecionar em nossa jornada cristã. O mesmo se aplica às nossas ações, ao nosso trabalho para o Senhor. Podemos querer fazer o bem, mas se Ele não nos impulsionou, estamos operando fora da Sua iniciativa e acabaremos tocando na morte espiritual. Não existem mercadorias espirituais, apenas a expressão simples e espontânea de Cristo; e somente Cristo.

Quando viemos a Deus pela primeira vez, uma obra profunda aconteceu em nossas vidas: nos foi mostrado que precisávamos de Cristo, e não de atos religiosos. Fomos salvos pela graça, por meio da fé Nele, e não pelo nosso grande esforço. Esta foi a primeira e gloriosa revelação, que destruiu de forma perfeita a nossa dependência do pecado e da autojustificação.

Agora, Deus nos convida a uma segunda revelação, igualmente profunda, que traz ainda maior descanso: o que precisamos é de Cristo, e não de coisas espirituais.

Se você está vivendo a vida pela sua própria força, você, na verdade, não precisa do poder da cruz. Mas se você está comprometido a viver pela Pessoa de Cristo, você abraçará a cruz diariamente.

Assim como um dia tivemos que largar os nossos pecados — orgulho, inveja, um temperamento explosivo — para recebê-Lo, agora devemos permitir que a estrutura espiritual da nossa santidade humana seja "destruída" para que Cristo possa realmente se tornar o nosso tudo. Podemos ser verdadeiramente pacientes, sinceramente humildes e excepcionalmente bons em nossa conduta, ganhando altas notas pelos padrões humanos. Mas este é o ponto crucial: se essas virtudes se originam em nós — se são o produto do nosso esforço, da nossa disciplina religiosa ou do nosso desenvolvimento de caráter *separado* do fluxo contínuo da Sua vida — elas são meramente coisas espirituais.

E uma coisa espiritual, por mais bonita que seja, se não originou em Cristo, é em última análise, inanimada.

Esta obra mais profunda de Deus não é sobre se tornar uma pessoa desvirtuada; é sobre se tornar uma pessoa livre. É um convite para ser libertado da pressão esmagadora de manter a nossa própria bondade. É um convite para parar de construir um currículo espiritual impressionante e, em vez disso, simplesmente entender, no íntimo do nosso ser, que Cristo é a nossa vida e o nosso tudo. Este é um Cristianismo vitorioso, completamente diferente da fé baseada em performance que o mundo frequentemente concebe.

Quem Toca em Cristo Toca a Própria Vida

Essa verdade se torna maravilhosamente prática em nosso dia a dia.

Deixe-me compartilhar uma experiência simples que ilustra este princípio claramente. Houve uma situação na vida de um amigo que exigia uma visita — o "dever cristão" era claro, o ato de compaixão era óbvio. Então, eu parti, motivado por um desejo de ser prestativo e amoroso. Contudo, quanto mais eu andava, mais pesado e frio meu espírito ficava. Toda a alegria espiritual se esvaiu.

Por quê? Porque percebi imediatamente que minha motivação havia mudado. Eu estava tentando realizar um ato de amor compassivo por minha própria conta. A ação em si era louvável e correta — visitar um amigo é uma coisa boa! — mas por eu estar fazendo, era uma "coisa" que eu havia fabricado, e eu encontrei instantaneamente a morte espiritual. O resultado daquela tarefa iniciada por mim mesmo teria sido um congelamento interior, um ato de compaixão sem a vida de

Cristo nele.

Esta é a lição vital para todos nós: Quando você toca em Cristo, você toca na vida; quando você toca apenas na conduta, você encontrará a morte.

Precisamos permitir que a Cruz de Cristo toque não apenas nosso comportamento, mas também nossa motivação. O Cristianismo não é um inventário complexo de bons itens que você coleta ou faz. Você poderia compilar cada gota de humildade, paciência e boas obras na terra, e ainda assim não teria a realidade de uma vida cristã. Isso porque Cristo, a Fonte viva, estaria faltando.

A gloriosa simplicidade é esta: Tudo o que Cristo dá é, na realidade, o Seu próprio Ser.

- Ele não apenas te concede paciência; Ele é a sua Paciência habitando em você.
- Ele não apenas te provê justiça; Ele é a sua Justiça que te torna completamente aceitável a Deus.
- Ele não apenas te oferece vida; Ele é a sua Vida fluindo sem esforço através de você.

-

Quando vivemos nossas vidas diante de Deus e confiamos nas 'coisas' — nossa própria bondade, nossa própria sabedoria, nossos próprios esforços — tocamos na morte porque Cristo não é a fonte. Mas no momento em que estendemos a mão em fé simples e tocamos o próprio Cristo, encontramos imediatamente a vida — vida vibrante, eterna e abundante, porque Ele mesmo é a Vida.

Liberdade: Trocando o Esforço pela Vida de Cristo

É uma experiência bastante familiar para aqueles que amam a Deus sinceramente: nós nos propomos a servi-Lo, querendo fazer mais e viver uma vida que O honre de verdade. Na superfície, nossas tarefas são excelentes, exigindo até sacrifício, sofrimento e o nosso melhor. Esperamos nos sentir vivos, realizados e abençoados neste serviço a Deus.

No entanto, muitos de nós temos enfrentado uma contradição intrigante e dolorosa. Apesar da nossa dedicação genuína e boas intenções, às vezes nos sentimos completamente esgotados, enfraquecidos e estranhamente reprovados interiormente. Em vez de tocar na vibrante vida espiritual, sentimos como se tivéssemos tocado em um vazio gélido — uma espécie de morte espiritual. Nossa consciência interna, que assumimos que deveria nos incomodar apenas quando pecamos, surpreendentemente nos censura quando estamos tentando fazer algo bom.

Quando você toca em Cristo, você toca na vida; quando você toca apenas na conduta, você encontrará a morte.

Onde erramos? O erro não estava na *ação* em si, mas na *fonte*. Aconteceu no momento em que concebemos a ideia de que a força, a sabedoria e a energia para servir a Deus deveriam se originar *em nós*. Confiamos na nossa capacidade de fabricar uma "boa obra" e, nesse esforço autoimposto, encontramos instantaneamente o esgotamento espiritual. É realmente uma realidade reveladora e séria: às vezes, recebemos uma correção interna mais nítida e dolorosa do Senhor pelo nosso bem iniciado por nós mesmos do que pelo nosso fracasso, porque o primeiro se disfarça como a Sua vontade quando está, na verdade, enraizado no eu.

É por isso que o princípio diante de Deus não é a **Árvore do Conhecimento do Bem e do Mal**, mas a **Árvore da Vida**.

A Árvore do Conhecimento do Bem e do Mal representa qualquer ação — até mesmo moral, religiosa ou louvável — que é realizada com base em nossa própria avaliação, força ou capacidade. Seu fruto, não importa quão "bom" pareça ao nosso ego, leva à morte espiritual porque é uma vida vivida **separada de Cristo** como a única Fonte. É um fundamento inadequado porque toda a questão do Cristianismo não é uma questão de moralidade ou performance; **é uma questão de vida em si.**

Uma notícia maravilhosa é que **a Árvore da Vida está viva!**

Esta é a nossa verdade libertadora: O desejo mais profundo de Deus é que você saia da esteira do esforço próprio. Ele não é apenas nosso Juiz quando pecamos; Aquele que vive em nós, o Espírito Santo, é também nosso amável Guia que nos redirecionará quando tentarmos fazer a Sua obra por meio da nossa própria força. Ele nos repreende, não para condenar, mas para nos resgatar da fraqueza e do vazio da bondade humana.

Seu trabalho não é lutar para ser bom, mas simplesmente **se conectar** — permanecer em Cristo, que é a sua vida. Tudo o que é bom, verdadeiro e vivificante flui apenas Dele. Toda vez que você escolhe conscientemente extrair sua motivação e força de Cristo, você toca na vida. Este é o caminho de Deus sem esforço, frutífero e eterno, onde o seu serviço espiritual não é mais um dever exaustivo, mas um gostoso transbordar do Cristo vivo em você.

Coisas Espirituais são Limitadas, Cristo é Ilimitado

Qual é o objeto da nossa busca espiritual mais intensa? Para muitos, é a procura por uma coisa — uma virtude específica ou uma qualidade espiritual que parece estar faltando em suas vidas.

Por exemplo, há inúmeros cristãos sinceros que expressam um desejo profundo, quase desesperado, por paciência. Muitas vezes, eles se sentem profundamente frustrados com sua natureza de temperamento rápido, desejando sinceramente uma solução instantânea. O pensamento implícito é: "Se eu pudesse simplesmente ser paciente... se Deus me desse uma 'dose de paciência' para engolir, então tudo estaria bem." Eles buscam a paciência como se fosse uma receita espiritual ou uma espécie de remédio emocional.

A desafiadora realidade dessa mentalidade é que qualquer coisa que você possa *contar* ou *adquirir* acabará por se esgotar. Você pode até conseguir manter essa "paciência de fonte própria" por alguns dias ou até uma semana, mas por ser meramente uma coisa — um produto temporário da força de vontade humana — ela tem um prazo de validade. Eventualmente, essa reserva emocional se esvai, e a paciência desaparece por completo. Se uma virtude é apenas um item que você possui, mesmo que tenha sido obtida por meio de uma oração sincera, ela será exaurida, e você se encontrará de volta ao ponto de partida.

Em Sua graça sem limites, Deus é compassivo e, por um breve período, Ele pode acomodar a necessidade temporária e a "insensatez" de Seus filhos, respondendo a orações por essas coisas específicas. Ele nos ajuda em nossa sinceridade inicial. No entanto, Ele não permitirá que essa condição se prolongue indefinidamente. Por quê?

A razão gloriosa e libertadora é esta: No plano supremo e na Palavra de Deus, não existe uma "coisa" separada à parte de Cristo — Cristo é tudo em todos.

Deus não permitirá que a paciência, a humildade ou mesmo o amor existam nesta terra como uma coisa autossustentável, pois Ele pretende redirecionar a nossa atenção da dádiva para Aquele que a dá. Ao deixarmos nossas coisas autossustentáveis na cruz, pois elas estão mortas, Ele nos revelará que Cristo é a Paciência, Cristo é a Humildade e Cristo é o Amor. É a Pessoa de Cristo, e não um item impessoal ou uma mercadoria espiritual, que Ele nos concede.

Quando o nosso relacionamento com o Senhor for verdadeiramente "normalizado" — quando pararmos de buscar traços espirituais como itens separados e reconhecermos que Cristo é a própria Fonte — descobriremos que todos os nossos problemas pessoais são resolvidos sem esforço. Fundamentalmente, a questão nunca é paciência, caráter ou qualquer outra qualidade. A questão é inteiramente Cristo.

Assim que a nossa dependência em Cristo for totalmente restaurada à realidade dinâmica que Deus projetou, a nossa multidão de problemas será devidamente resolvida. A questão total e abrangente de nossa vida cristã, vitória e caráter é Cristo, e não uma coleção de coisas. Descanse Nele, pois Ele é tudo de que você precisa.

Deus Pai, eu me coloco diante de Ti agora para aceitar e abraçar de todo o coração a profunda realidade da cruz de Cristo. Eu recebo a gloriosa verdade de que a jornada da minha vida está centrada na Tua vontade de convergir todas as coisas em Jesus.

Eu confesso que a obra da cruz não é meramente um evento histórico do qual eu me lembro, mas um evento diário que eu abraço, e recebo o seu poder transformador contínuo em mim. Eu aceito que na cruz, Cristo declarou: "Está consumado" (João 19:30), e é nessa obra consumada que a minha vida real começa e tem fim.

Eu não confio mais no meu próprio esforço, mas no Seu sacrifício supremo, vendo ali o próprio coração do Teu amor, da Tua graça salvadora e a chave para a mais profunda revelação da Sua identidade.

Eu abraço a verdade de que já morri para a minha velha vida e rendo o meu velho eu, sabendo que a minha nova e real vida está escondida em segurança com Cristo.

Eu Te agradeço porque Cristo é a própria fonte da minha força e do meu propósito, e eu descanso confiantemente na verdade de que Ele é a minha Santificação, não um processo, mas uma Pessoa sendo vivida através de mim. Eu declaro que não possuo nada além de Cristo e, Nele, eu tenho tudo.

Eu escolho permanecer na verdade libertadora da cruz, onde minha vida começa e tem fim. Amém!

8

Precisamos Conhecer Cristo

A grande e singular verdade no coração da nossa caminhada com Deus é esta: Cada questão, cada desafio e cada vitória giram em torno de uma magnífica proposição — **o profundo e pessoal conhecimento de Jesus Cristo.**

O que significa verdadeiramente "conhecer Cristo"? É muito mais do que concordar com um conjunto de ideias ou ter uma teologia correta. É uma experiência **ativa, substancial e totalmente pessoal**. Para alguns, eles O conhecem como o Seu amor sem limites; para outros, eles O conhecem como a Sua humildade perfeita, a Sua paciência sem fim ou a Sua paz inabalável. A medida da nossa vida espiritual é precisamente a medida em que descobrimos que Cristo é a corporificação de todas essas "coisas" necessárias. Este — e somente este — é o conhecimento apropriado e vital do nosso Salvador.

Conhecê-Lo é vê-Lo não como um ajudador distante, mas como

a **nossa realidade viva**.

Pense nesse momento de testemunho genuíno e transformador. Alguém que antes se sentia completamente consumido por uma imundície interior — cujos pensamentos, coração e hábitos eram uma bagunça — agora pode se levantar e declarar: "Eu agradeço a Deus, Cristo se tornou a minha pureza." Não foi um impulso repentino de força de vontade ou um programa de autoajuda que os consertou. Foi um momento de profunda revelação espiritual que lhes mostrou: **Esta pureza não é uma coisa que eu possuo; é o próprio Cristo habitando em mim.** Este é o segredo do Cristianismo: Cristo não é um hóspede passivo; Ele é a Vida que, por Sua presença, traz consigo toda virtude espiritual. Não se trata do que é do seu eu natural; trata-se do que Ele traz para dentro de você.

A Distinção Crucial: Vida vs. Morte

Com esta poderosa verdade em mente, devemos olhar para a nossa própria vida espiritual com honestidade. Devo declarar isso claramente e com profundo amor: um filho de Deus cujos olhos espirituais ainda não foram abertos para ver Cristo como tudo em sua vida — como a sua própria fonte de vida para tudo — está, em um sentido profundo, limitado na sua utilidade para Deus. Por quê? Porque o que lhe resta são simplesmente as suas próprias boas obras e o esforço humano.

Cada questão, cada desafio e cada vitória giram em torno de uma magnífica proposição — o profundo e pessoal conhecimento de Jesus Cristo.

Você pode orar fervorosamente e receber a graça momentânea de Deus, mas se o resultado final for meramente uma "coisa" — um sentimento temporário de paz ou um breve lampejo de paciência — está fadado a ser passageiro e terá pouco ou nenhum valor espiritual eterno diante de Deus. Devemos encarar a triste realidade de que grande parte da graça que as pessoas recebem hoje é experimentada como um objeto, uma solução temporária.

No entanto, existe uma diferença bela e vitoriosa. Alguns crentes recebem a graça com uma Personalidade: a sua graça não é um conceito abstrato, mas é o próprio Filho de Deus. Eu anseio pelo dia em que você possa declarar a Deus com alegre confiança: "Pai, eu Te agradeço e Te louvo, porque a graça que recebi não é um sentimento ou uma fórmula; a minha graça é uma Pessoa, que tem uma Personalidade — **é Cristo.**"

No momento em que você vê esta diferença, pode distinguir instantaneamente a vida da morte. Infelizmente, muitos cristãos sinceros são capazes apenas de discernir entre o bem e o mal; eles não conseguem diferenciar entre a vida e a morte. Eles falham em ver que tudo na economia espiritual está contido em Cristo. Ele é tanto o objetivo final quanto o meio para alcançá-lo. No reino espiritual autêntico e vibrante, não há "coisa" nem "assunto", **há somente Cristo.**

O Toque Espiritual da Morte nas "Boas" Coisas

Uma vez que Deus abre verdadeiramente os seus olhos para esta realidade, você passa a discernir espiritualmente o seu dia a dia. Você começa a reconhecer as **coisas espirituais** — virtudes geradas pelo esforço próprio — sempre que as encontra. Isso pode parecer estranho no início, mas é intrinsecamente real e libertador.

Você pode conhecer uma pessoa que é excepcionalmente paciente, gentil, humilde, amorosa e generosa. Ela é um modelo de virtude! No entanto, para alguém cujos olhos foram abertos, essa pessoa é meramente "cheia de coisas". Assim como você pode facilmente notar a diferença entre um casaco e a pessoa que o veste, você agora pode diferenciar um traço religioso externo do Cristo que habita em você.

A verdade crítica e desafiadora é esta: **Tudo o que pertence às "coisas" está morto por dentro e produz morte por fora.**

Se uma pessoa opera a partir de uma bondade gerada por si mesma, ela pode ser muito agradável, mas sua influência é limitada ao simples reino humano do bem e do mal; ela não tem um efeito espiritual verdadeiro e transformador. Uma pessoa que é naturalmente bem-humorada, perseverante e amorosa pode agradar você imensamente, mas se essas características são apenas traços da sua carne, elas, surpreendentemente, despertarão em você um fraco, mas inconfundível, **senso de morte**. O seu espírito, estando vivo em Cristo, não pode abraçar uma obra morta, e uma resistência interna será percebida.

Todos nós já sentimos isso. Às vezes, em uma reunião de oração, uma oração é tão cheia da vida de Cristo que você grita espontaneamente: "Amém!", porque seu espírito foi profundamente tocado pela Vida. Mas outra oração, embora eloquente e fervorosa, deixa você com um vazio gélido. Você sente o desejo de que ela acabe, porque a oração parece uma extensão da personalidade da pessoa — uma "coisa" de esforço próprio que carrega o toque da morte. Uma coisa feita pelo esforço do homem produz morte espiritual não apenas na pessoa que o faz, mas também naqueles ao seu redor, pois não há absolutamente nenhum valor espiritual no que é feito apenas pelo homem.

Cristo é a Nossa Vitória: O Fim das Nossas Obras

Reconhecendo que esta é a situação que nos encontramos — onde qualquer coisa proveniente do nosso próprio esforço carrega o "toque da morte" — somos conduzidos ao único caminho viável diante de Deus: **esperar Nele e cessar as nossas próprias obras.**

À medida que somos verdadeiramente guiados pelo Espírito Santo, faremos uma descoberta surpreendente: **Deus odeia as obras iniciadas em nosso "eu" tanto quanto odeia os nossos pecados.** Para aqueles que cometem pecados, o salário é a morte. Para aqueles que confiam no seu próprio desempenho religioso, eles não conseguem se libertar da sua própria vida do "eu". Deus rejeita profundamente as nossas obras assim como repudia os nossos pecados.

Apenas uma coisa é aceita por Deus, e essa é o Seu Filho, Jesus Cristo. **É Cristo quem se torna todas as coisas para nós.** Este é o grande alívio e a vitória máxima! Não é "eu tentando ser humilde", mas **Ele Se humilhando** em mim. Não é "eu lutando para amar", mas **Ele amando** em meu lugar. Ele não me dá apenas poder; **Ele mesmo é o meu Poder.**

Para aqueles que acabaram de ser salvos, por favor, compreendam isso o mais cedo possível! **Quando você é liberto da busca por coisas espirituais, você finalmente tocará o próprio Senhor Jesus.** Quanto mais tempo você viver no "monte de coisas" que precisa, mais difícil se torna a libertação. Pode ser que Deus, em Seu profundo amor, o faça passar por um processo doloroso de quebra e de revelação das suas próprias limitações para lhe tirar esses itens originados em você mesmo, para que finalmente você fique desesperado o suficiente para receber Cristo como o seu tudo.

---

*Apenas uma coisa é aceita por Deus, e essa é o Seu Filho, Jesus Cristo. **É Cristo quem se torna todas as coisas para nós.** Este é o grande alívio e a vitória máxima!*

Anelamos o dia glorioso em que todas as coisas — no céu e na terra — serão convergidas em Cristo. Mas deixe-me desafiá-lo hoje: **Como você pode esperar que Cristo seja tudo naquele dia futuro se você não O conhece como o seu**

tudo hoje? Agora mesmo, Cristo está pronto para ser todas as nossas coisas. Deus nos deu o Seu próprio Filho; Ele nos deu a Si mesmo. Portanto, Cristo deve ser o nosso tudo em todos hoje. Não há distinção entre Cristo e as coisas espirituais. Nada é espiritual, **somente Cristo é.**

Que esta realidade comece a se evidenciar poderosamente em sua vida agora mesmo. Declare hoje que Cristo é seu tudo em tudo: "Ele está na minha paciência! Ele está na minha gentileza! Ele está no meu amor! Pois Ele é meu tudo!" Esperamos com alegria aquele dia em que o Filho de Deus Se manifestará para ser tudo e em todos, mas as lições que aprendemos hoje são as experiências que nos preparam para essa manifestação completa. Deus o abençoe enquanto você descansa e vive Nele.

Vamos Orar !

Deus Pai, nós nos achegamos humildemente à Tua presença, reconhecendo a nossa profunda e constante necessidade da Tua graça. Senhor, confessamos que a nossa visão espiritual frequentemente não é nítida. Olhamos para o mundo ao nosso redor, e as "coisas" desta vida parecem intensamente reais e urgentes. E ao mesmo tempo, Tu, Cristo Jesus, o próprio centro de toda a realidade, pode nos parecer distante e abstrato. Muitas vezes, conhecemos os conceitos do Cristianismo, mas falhamos em Te conhecer verdadeiramente. Oramos com toda sinceridade, Senhor, abre os nossos olhos!

Concede-nos uma visão divina que penetre o véu do material e do meramente religioso. Pedimos que Cristo se torne tão vivamente real para nós que tudo o mais — toda a nossa busca, todo o esforço próprio, toda nossa desordem espiritual — se desvaneça. E deixe que as coisas passageiras desta vida percam o seu domínio, e que a Tua vida abundante e vibrante preencha cada canto do nosso ser.

Pai, oramos sinceramente pela libertação da tirania da "Árvore do Conhecimento". Liberta-nos da mentalidade que vê o crescimento espiritual como virtudes que devemos adquirir. E em vez de perseguir qualidades abstratas, ensina-nos a simplesmente conhecer e nos relacionar com o Senhor, que é uma Pessoa. Que Tu, o Cristo Vivo, se torne a realidade que abrange tudo, que define e substitui todos os "frutos do bem" que erroneamente buscamos.

Estabelece uma conexão tão profunda que as pessoas não vejam o nosso esforço, mas vejam Cristo em nós. Ajuda-nos a compreender o magnífico contraste entre uma vida enraizada no Teu Filho e uma baseada nos nossos próprios esforços. Reconhecemos que o verdadeiro crescimento requer o quebrantamento da nossa autossuficiência. Nós nos rendemos a este processo necessário. Faz-nos entender quão diferente é o caminho da verdadeira vida cristã de qualquer mera imitação ou falso substituto.

Não permitas que nos enganemos, acreditando que estamos cheios de vida quando estamos apenas cheios das nossas próprias "coisas" mortas. Pedimos o Teu toque poderoso, Senhor. Faz residência permanente em nós, para que, vindo do íntimo do nosso ser para fora, seja Cristo e somente Cristo.

Por fim, oramos uma bênção sobre esta mensagem e cada palavra dita, para que Tu a uses para trazer inúmeros corações de volta à singular Pessoa do Teu Filho, o todo suficiente. Onde a fraqueza humana falha e as nossas próprias palavras são insuficientes, que o Teu Espírito Santo fale. Pedimos que Tu redimas a nossa tolice e uses este momento para trazer glória ao Teu Nome. Que este seja um dia de profunda exposição espiritual para muitos, onde toda falsidade seja desmascarada, e Tu, Cristo Jesus, sejas claramente distinguido de todos os substitutos feitos pelo homem. Abençoa a Tua própria Palavra e glorifica o Teu Nome, pois em nome do Senhor Jesus, nós cremos e oramos. Amém!

Sobre o Autor

A minha jornada com Deus começou com uma percepção profunda e transformadora: Deus estava pessoalmente em busca de mim, ainda que eu não O buscasse. Ele me quis antes mesmo de eu O desejar. Essa descoberta me levou à verdade libertadora de que a fé cristã não é uma lista de tarefas religiosas, mas um relacionamento íntimo e crescente com a Pessoa viva de Jesus Cristo.

Em minha caminhada com Jesus, encontrei uma esperança e uma liberdade que aumentam a cada dia. Elas não são um fogo passageiro que se apaga com o tempo, mas uma chama acesa em meu coração. Por isso, minha paixão é compartilhar que Cristo não é apenas uma parte da vida, mas a provisão absoluta e total para ela; é n'Ele que toda a verdade e propósito residem eternamente.

Diariamente, com essa chama acesa, eu e minha esposa moramos no Norte da Califórnia, onde servimos em uma igreja local.

Para mais informações, por favor, envie um email para hgsouza@freetosetfree.com.